Harriett,

Thank you so very much for all the support and love. And most of all the prayers which have helped through this very difficult year. You are very special! You are very special!

May our Father bless you richly because of Jesus Christ

Love,
Alice Spring

25 Dec 1997

BECAUSE *He* LIVES

*The Stories and Inspiration
Behind the Songs of
Bill and Gloria Gaither*

GLORIA GAITHER

ZondervanPublishingHouse
Grand Rapids, Michigan

A Division of HarperCollins*Publishers*

Requests for information should be addressed to:

ZondervanPublishingHouse
Grand Rapids, Michigan 49530

Library of Congress Cataloging-in-Publication Data

Gaither, Gloria.
　　　Because he lives: the stories and inspiration behind the songs of Bill and Gloria Gaither / Gloria Gaither.
　　　　　p.　　cm.
　　　Rev. and expanded version of the 1977 ed.
　　　ISBN: 0-310-21310-X (pbk.)
　　　　　1. Gaither, Gloria.　2. Gaither, Bill.　3. Gospel musicians—United States—Biography
　　I. Title.
　　ML420.G13A3　　1997
　　782.24'4'092273—dc 21　　　　　　　　　　　　　　　　　　　　　　　97-35858
　　[B]　　　　　　　　　　　　　　　　　　　　　　　　　　　　　　　　　CIP
　　　　　　　　　　　　　　　　　　　　　　　　　　　　　　　　　　　　MN

Page 164. From *Our Town* by Thornton Wilder. © Copyright 1938 by Coward McCann, Inc. All rights reserved. Reprinted by permission.

Page 14. "The Words and the Music." Lyric by Suzanne Gaither Jennings. Music by Jeff Silvey. © Copyright 1990 Townsend and Warbucks Music and Riverstone Music. All rights reserved.

Page 33. From *There Is a Hope* by Laura Lee Oldham and Doug Oldham. © Copyright 1996 by Laura Lee Oldham and Doug Oldham. Published by Fleming H. Revell (a division of Baker Book House Company). All rights reserved. Used by permission.

Page 79. From "Christ Arose!" Words and music by Robert Lowry. Used by permission.

Page 79. From "He Lives!" Words and music by Alfred H. Ackley. ©1933 by Homer A. Rodeheaver. © Copyright renewed 1961 by The Rodehearer Company (a div. of Word Music). All rights reserved. Used by permission.

This edition printed on acid-free paper and meets the American National Standards Institute Z39.48 standard.

All Scripture quotations, unless otherwise indicated, are taken from the *Holy Bible: New International Version*®. NIV®. Copyright © 1973, 1978, 1984 by International Bible Society. Used by permission of Zondervan Publishing House. All rights reserved.

Published in association with the literary agency of Alive Communications, Inc., 1465 Kelly Johnson Blvd. #320, Colorado Springs, CO 80920.

Interior design by Sherri L. Hoffman

Printed in the United States of America

97 98 99 00 01 02 03 04 /❖ DC/ 10 9 8 7 6 5 4 3 2 1

To those great writers like
Stuart Hamblen,
Ira Stanphill,
Fanny Crosby,
Mosie Lister,
and Annie Johnson Flint,
who showed us the power of the right
words married to the right music.

Contents

Foreword		7
Introduction		11
1.	Because He Lives	16
2.	God Gave the Song	26
3.	He Touched Me	30
4.	I Believe in a Hill Called Mount Calvary	38
5.	Going Home	44
6.	Since Jesus Passed By	48
7.	The Longer I Serve Him	54
8.	There's Something About That Name	60
9.	Let's Just Praise the Lord	66
10.	Something Beautiful	70
11.	The Family of God	76
12.	The King Is Coming	82
13.	The Old Rugged Cross Made the Difference	88
14.	I Could Never Outlove the Lord	94
15.	The Church Triumphant	98
16.	Jesus Is Lord of All	102
17.	It's Beginning to Rain	108
18.	Gentle Shepherd	112
19.	It Is Finished	118
20.	We Have This Moment, Today	126
21.	Joy Comes in the Morning	132

22. That's Worth Everything   136
23. These Are They   140
24. I Am Loved   146
25. Go Ask   152
26. We Are So Blessed   156
27. Fully Alive   160
28. Upon This Rock   166
29. The Stage Is Bare   172
30. Broken and Spilled Out   176
31. Praise You   180
32. I've Just Seen Jesus   186
33. Sinner Saved by Grace   192
34. Unshakable Kingdom   198
35. Peace Be Still   202
36. Tell Me   206
37. I Don't Belong   210
38. Loving God, Loving Each Other   216
    Credits   221

Foreword by Three Friends

I was swamped in the sixties ... traveling and singing with the Billy Graham Crusades took all the time I had to offer. Across my desk came many letters and inquisitions from hopeful gospel music artists wanting our advice or recognition for the songs they had written or sung. With so many sincere submissions but so little time, my stack of correspondence grew tall, yet I did not want to send an impersonal form letter and was teased for being such a "softy." Even with the best intentions of personally responding, often there were letters left unanswered.

On my desk, tossed somewhere among the many other letters that accompanied it, was a certain letter from two young writers from Indiana with a new song, "He Touched Me," written by the young husband. It was mimeographed and handwritten on staff paper. Several years later I found myself in the heart of Nashville, Tennessee, with the honor of presenting Bill Gaither the Dove Award for Song of the Year for—behold—the tremendously loved, "He Touched Me"! You can imagine my astonishment to learn of what I had missed ... yet what the world captured for me. Since then, I have sung and recorded "He Touched Me" and many others of Bill and Gloria's inspired songs, often with a smile upon my face as I think of how God ordains our lives in such a divine fashion and how *He* will let *His* song be heard.

— George Beverly Shea
Beloved soloist for the Billy Graham Crusades

*W*hen I was nine years old, I made my first album. Actually, it wasn't much. Mama and Daddy were afraid that when my voice changed I wouldn't be able to sing anymore, so they took me down to a recording studio in Houston and my singing career began. The title of that recording was "He Touched Me." I was a little kid singing some pretty grown-up songs.

I've sung the songs of Bill and Gloria Gaither all my life — and, in the past few years, I've had a privilege of singing their songs with them. I've learned these great songs have great stories behind them. When I was a kid, I didn't know there *were* stories behind songs. I knew the songs I sang were pretty, and I knew people would cry or shout when I sang them. But I didn't know why people responded the way they did; I didn't understand that they were seeing their lives in the song.

Today, as a writer, I love to hear the stories behind the songs. I want to know what brings people to the place in their lives where they can say, "Because He lives, I can face tomorrow" or "The longer I serve Him, the sweeter He grows" or "Hold on my child, joy comes in the morning."

Now I'm thirty-nine and I, too, have a story. It's pretty much the same story as Bill and Gloria Gaither's — "I'm just a sinner saved by grace." I'm so grateful they have been able to put my story, and yours too perhaps, into a song.

— Mark Lowry
Comedian, recording artist,
and member of the Gaither Vocal Band

*W*e were all young when we first met, midway through the turbulent sixties. Bill and Gloria Gaither were high school teachers in Bill's hometown — a small, rural, central Indiana town so quiet you could hear the corn grow. I was a Massachusetts-bred, New York-trained college music professor who had earlier come to Nashville, Tennessee, to manage the Nashville Symphony Orchestra and had recently joined the fledgling Benson Publishing Company as "creative director" — a pretentious title of my own choosing, offered to compensate for my very modest salary.

I learned that Bill had sung around the Midwest on the weekends with his sister, Mary Ann, and brother, Dan, a uniquely wonderful singer. The Gaither Trio sang an easy-rhythm kind of music — deeply rooted in Southern gospel but with all of the franticness removed. Their harmony was smooth, warm, gentle, and encouraging. Bill had a heart for worship and was writing a few of his own songs for this family trio to sing. ("I've Been to Calvary" was one of his first to be recorded by other artists, along with others including "The Joy of Serving the Lord" and "Lovest Thou Me?" Later, after Bill and Gloria were married and writing songs together, he would write both the music and lyrics to "He Touched Me," a song that remains, to this day, one of worldwide Christendom's most beloved testimony expressions.)

In 1962 Bill had met and married a young French and English teacher who began singing in the trio with Bill and his brother Danny. To the smooth trio harmony Gloria brought the new dimension of her deeply moving narrations like "There's Something About That Name" and the powerful, challenging "Church Triumphant." Producing the Gaither Trio recordings of that decade-plus period was one of the greatest joys and privileges of my life.

I don't know exactly when Bill first started seeking Gloria's critique on his latest song lyric, or when she began writing the lyrics to the music Bill was creating and the ideas they were discussing together. I do know that it was an historic encounter that signaled the beginning of a more than thirty-year-long songwriting partnership that has given the church of Jesus Christ words and music to express the deepest cries of our hearts, the aching needs of our psyche, the joys and despairs as well as the failures and triumphs of our spirits . . . and praise and adoration for the God who is at work in it all.

I am a truly blessed man! I have been given one of the best seats in the house to watch this piece of history joyously unfold. I often heard the songs first — the ink hardly dry — as we prepared for Gaither Trio recordings. I saw Bill and Gloria at close range as they lived amazingly simple lives in that small Indiana town, as they struggled to translate the call of the God of the Universe into the daily challenge of raising a family in an often hard world with real-life problems and real-life opportunities. I've seen them — week after week, month after month, year after year — finding God faithful and sufficient in it all. I've watched them chronicle their spiritual journey into this rich treasury of gospel songs that have informed and illuminated our spiritual trek. And I've seen them, rather reluctantly, leave their life in Alexandria to travel to a hundred cities across America and Canada to share, through their songs, their experience with a real God working with real people like us.

They have taught us to sing — and live — "Because He lives, I can face tomorrow!"

— Robert MacKenzie
Music executive and long-term producer for the Bill Gaither Trio

Introduction

$\mathcal{L}$ ooking as professional as I could, I hurried out of room 112 and down the hall toward the front office to drop off the day's attendance sheet. I was a bit rattled by my first day as a new substitute teacher. I had walked into the classroom that morning just as a 6-foot-4-inch basketball player threw a typewriter over the heads of the other students to his buddy on the other side of the room.

I had stared for a moment in amazement, then cleared my throat and, in the most commanding voice I could muster, said, "The class will come to order. In your seats, please." Much to my surprise and relief, the class of high school seniors responded and gave me their attention.

I was nineteen years old and a junior at Anderson College. My French professor had called me into her office and asked if I'd be willing to share with another student the class load of an area high school French teacher who was scheduled for cancer surgery during Christmas vacation. I would start teaching three of her classes at the beginning of the second semester.

I was almost to the office that Monday when a young man with a funny looking crew cut came around the corner and dropped his pencil in front of me. He stopped to pick it up, looked up at me, and said, "Hello, there. What is your name?"

"Gloria Sickal," I answered. "Who are you?"

"My name is Bill Gaither, and I teach English. I've been teaching junior high English for three years, but I just started here this week as head of the department."

"Oh, yes," I said. "Bill Gaither. You're the one who has a brother that my friend is dying to meet."

"That's the story of my life," Bill responded. "Everyone wants to meet my brother."

I never got around to introducing Bill's brother to my friend, but Bill and I did begin to talk in the high school hallways about politics and literature and our love for the Lord. He took me to lunch and to a few Indiana basketball games.

When Bill Gaither finally got the courage to play me a couple of gospel songs he'd written, we were already planning to be married. By then, too, I had gotten up the nerve to show him some of my poetry.

Neither of us would have believed it then if someone had told us we'd spend the rest of our lives writing songs together. We did know that Bill's boyhood dream of singing in a gospel quartet had been crushed by failure his first year of high school, a failure that, thankfully, sent him to college and then to a master's degree for teaching English. And my early love for writing and speaking had been laid aside to major in French, English, and sociology in preparation for becoming a missionary — perhaps to Africa.

The day we walked down the aisle of the church my father once pastored to join our lives in marriage, we both knew, too, that wherever life took us, we had each found a soul mate who could understand our passions for great ideas and eternal truths that could change lives and shape destinies.

At first, even before we were married, I began "fixing" the lyrics to Bill's songs — giving him a line here, a phrase there, an ending or an opener. But gradually, we began to develop a system that almost always involved us both searching for the right way to express — Bill in music, I in words — a great idea that would not be silenced. It was the idea that drove us both — always the idea.

Sometimes our songs came directly from experiences we were having, people God brought into our lives, or situations through which God was teaching us. Other times songs simply came from insight from the Word, or a phrase from a sermon, or a sentence from a prayer. Off we would go in response to some revelation of God that was fresh and surprising to us, trying to find a way to express in words and music those things that really cannot be expressed in mere words.

Often we have been asked which comes first — the music or the words. There have been times when a whole lyric came to me in one piece to which Bill alone or with another musician wrote the music. More often he has had a musical setting to which I have written words. (I prefer to write to a setting — emotionally and artistically right for an idea.) But always the idea comes before either the music or the words.

It has been thirty-five years since we wrote our first songs together. The journey of our lives has been full of surprises and what we call "holy accidents" — accidents to us, but not to God. If our more than six hundred songs were now listed chronologically, they would chronicle a pilgrimage of growth and discovery. Those songs and the insights that precipitated them have opened the doors to other whole vocations: recording, giving concerts, starting musical events like Praise Gathering, Family Fest, Jubilate, and, most recently, whole series of gatherings with some pioneers and young artists we call our Homecoming Friends, captured on video for others to enjoy.

Writing songs, at first for our own children, has spawned many other projects such as musicals, recordings, and videos for children around the world.

All of these things have been exciting, but nothing is as exciting, even yet, as a great idea that finds lodging in our souls and then grows until it demands to be born in the form of a song — words and music.

God has bound our hearts to each other with the strong strands of thousands of phrases, thousands of lines, thousands of tunes, and then in turn tied us in love to all those whose voices have raised those songs like an incense to the throne of the Father.

A lyric our daughter Suzanne wrote seems to express this bond best:

> The words and the music
> The melody and rhyme
> Woven together, keeping in time;
> The words and the music,
> The voice and the pace
> Uniting our souls
> Through the long endless days.
>
> "The Words and the Music"
> —Suzanne Gaither Jennings

Because He Lives

God sent His Son; they called Him Jesus.
He came to love, heal and forgive —
He lived and died to buy my pardon;
An empty grave is there to prove my Savior lives.

Because He lives,
I can face tomorrow
Because He lives,
All fear is gone;
Because I know
He holds the future,
And life is worth the living
Just because He lives.

How sweet to hold our newborn baby
And feel the pride and joy he gives;
But greater still the calm assurance,
This child can face uncertain days because He lives.

And then one day I'll cross death's river;
I'll fight life's final war with pain —
And then as death gives way to victory,
I'll see the lights of glory and I'll know He reigns.

Because He lives,
I can face tomorrow
Because He lives,
All fear is gone;
Because I know
He holds the future,
And life is worth the living
Just because He lives.

Because He Lives

$\mathcal{B}$ill and I were married and started our family in the sixties. Suzanne was born in 1964; Amy came along in 1969. It was a turbulent decade. Racial tensions had torn the country apart. In Los Angeles, Watts had erupted in riots that nearly burned that part of the city to the ground. Civil rights activists had suffered and some had been killed as our country was forced to look at the gaping chasm between the celebrated American promise of freedom and the reality for many of its citizens.

The Vietnam conflict (we refused to call it a war) would drag on through three administrations and eighteen years, taking nearly 57,000 American lives. It would be the first war in our history in which there would be no winners. Young men had fled the country to avoid the draft. Many who stayed to serve were uncertain of America's objectives and would feel deserted themselves by the very citizens they marched off to defend.

A young generation of Americans felt disillusioned and unable to find answers to insistent questions few had previously dared to ask aloud. Many asked good questions about the materialistic lifestyle their Depression-era parents had relentlessly pursued, but few went to the right source for answers. "What's It All About?" was more than the name of a song; it was an unanswered question this generation drowned in alcohol and obliterated with drugs. New "designer drugs" concocted in laboratories began to surface. LSD and "angel dust" promised "a spiritual experience" and soon even a few college professors were giving these drugs to their students to "expand their minds" and broaden their horizon of experience.

The hippy generation felt increasingly estranged from society. While some took daring risks to get involved and make a difference, others chose to "get high" and "drop out." They called themselves flower children and advocated free love, yet all too often what they experienced was not so much love as deep disappointment and burned-out minds.

In this climate, Bill and I were writing songs about what we saw as real and lasting answers to the turmoil of the human spirit, about truths that had preceded us and would be around long after we were gone. On weekends, we would travel, singing our songs and sharing from our own daily experiences — how a deep commitment to the lordship of Christ had given us purpose, direction, and stability. Then, in the fall of 1969, several things happened to make us test the reality of our convictions.

Bill's sister, Mary Ann, went though a divorce that was devastating to her and to our whole family because it was the first time divorce had touched us so closely. We felt helpless to help her.

About this time we realized we were expecting another baby. Suzanne was four and Amy was three months old, and although we had always planned to have three, we were not expecting to have a baby so soon. My body had not quite recuperated from the last pregnancy. And Bill, about this same time, contracted mononucleosis, which left him exhausted and depressed.

Then a person close to us, whom we loved and in whom we had invested a great deal in terms of time and energy, asked us to financially support a project we felt was unwise. When we turned him down, he stormed through our home and shouted at Bill, "You're just a phony! You wouldn't believe this Jesus stuff if you weren't making your living at it!" He slammed the door and walked out of our lives.

I know of no one who searches his heart more deeply or questions his motives more often than Bill, but the person who is the most conscientious is often the most easily destroyed by unjust accusations. Already depleted and discouraged by the drain on his energies due to the mononucleosis and filled with anxiety by the world situation, Bill was thrown into deep depression and a time of self-analysis.

He would sit in a big chair in our family room and go over his life, his words, his actions, his motives. Could there be even a hint of truth to this man's accusations? Bill couldn't pray. And the long dark tunnel before him seemed to have no end.

Bill and I would talk about all the circumstances of the world, and about this new discouragement, and wind up saying, "If this world is like this now, what will it be in fifteen or sixteen years for our baby? What will this child face?" We were filled with fear and uncertainty.

One day a dear friend, Sid Guillen, came by the house. Knowing that Bill was feeling defeated, Sid had asked God to show him what to do, and it was obvious that he had heard from God when he walked into our family room. "This is not just discouragement, Bill," he said, "this is an imposition of Satan. I would like to anoint you with oil as the Scripture commands, and rebuke this spirit of fear in the name of Jesus." He proceeded to do just that, and then he gave us both a big hug and left.

Gradually, Bill felt better. Physically and spiritually he saw a growing ray of light in the darkness. Yet we worried about the world situation and about the baby I was carrying.

On New Year's Eve we were scheduled to sing, but a day before we were to leave, it began to snow — not a few flurries, but a major blizzard. The next morning the driveway was buried in a couple feet of snow and roads were impassable. Bill dug out the driveway and tried to get to the highway, but the state police turned him back, saying they were arresting anyone out driving, except for emergency vehicles. As I remember, it was the only time we ever missed a singing engagement because of the weather.

That evening I lay on the couch looking at a large piece of art my mother had painted in oils and given to us for Christmas. It depicted a farmer's hand, resting on an old fence post encircled with barbed wire. The farmer's hand was rough and cracked by years of digging in the soil. Dirt was under his fingernails. His palm held a mound of black rich soil from which sprouted a tiny seedling that he obviously intended to plant.

As I looked at Mother's painting, it seemed that God spoke to me in the silence: *Look at how fragile that seedling is. Think of all that could happen to it: flood, drought, pests, disease. But that seedling is going to make it. It will grow up straight and strong because of the tenderness of the farmer's hand. He knows the threats; he's committed to that plant, and he will take good care of it. One day it will bear a crop. It will not only live, it will thrive.*

Early that spring, that New Year's insight took on greater significance for me. The previous fall we had paved the parking lot behind our office. We had watched as the graders had prepared the bed. Then heavy rollers had embedded crushed stone into the surface. Next had come smaller crushed stone, then pea gravel, then sand. Each time the heavy rollers had stamped the layers down flat and smooth. Finally, the workmen had poured hot tar — blacktop — on all the prepared layers and rolled it again and again until it was packed, firm and smooth.

After the winter Bill's dad, George, came into the office. "Come over here a minute," he said to Bill and me, beckoning us outside. He was a quiet man of few words, so when he said something we listened. We followed him to the middle of the new parking lot. "Look there," he said, pointing at the pavement. There, poking up through all those layers of stone, sand, and blacktop, stood a tiny blade of green grass. George just grinned and walked back into the office, leaving us there to marvel at this amazing story of Easter from a tiny blade of grass. It was confirming a truth that had been pushing its way to the surface of our souls: Life wins! Life wins!

That summer, on July 19, I gave birth to a perfect, precious baby boy. After the winter of our discontent, this child seemed like the blade of grass pushing up through the pavement.

We hadn't written a song for what seemed like a very long time, but as that season of our lives ended, we would soon put words and music to what God was teaching us: It isn't because the world is stable that we have the courage to live our lives or start marriages or have children. The world has never been stable. Jesus Himself was born into the cruelest and most unstable of worlds. No, we have babies and keep trusting and risk living because the Resurrection is true! The Resurrection was not just a one-time event in history; it is a principle built into the very fabric of our beings, a fact reverberating from every cell of creation: Life wins! Life wins!

We took that little baby boy home. We named him Benjamin, "most beloved son." And a few weeks later this song poured from our hearts:

God sent His son; they called Him Jesus.
He came to love, heal and forgive;
He bled and died to buy my pardon —
An empty grave is there to prove my Savior lives.

How sweet to hold our newborn baby
And feel the pride and joy he gives;
But greater still, the calm assurance —
This child can face uncertain days because He lives.

This song took on even wider dimensions for me about five years later. About four o'clock one morning Bill and I, staying in a Kansas City motel, were awakened by a phone call. It was our pastor: "Gloria," he said, "I don't have very good news for you; your dad just passed away. Your mother got up to check on him and found him gone."

I couldn't believe it. Daddy had been seeing a doctor for congestion in his chest. The condition hadn't improved, and on Friday, before we left town, he had seen another doctor who had told him the congestion was not in his lungs but around his heart. On Monday he was to talk further about insertion of a pacemaker.

There were no words to express my grief. Bill held me as I wept silently until dawn. We flew home to Indiana to help Mother with arrangements and to explain Grandpa's death to our children, who were staying with my parents that weekend. I prayed that a little four-year-old boy, a five-year-old girl, and a daughter who would be nine in two days would somehow understand a bit of the promise of the Resurrection.

I went through that day acutely aware of every detail, yet mercifully numb to pain that waited on the edges of my consciousness, like wolves on the circumference of a campfire. I went with my mother to talk to the mortician. He took us into a big room filled with caskets of all types. He explained the advantages and drawbacks of each — walnut, mahogany, bronze. He showed us the linings — blue, peach, ivory; in satin, taffeta, velvet. My brain was exploding with the absurdity of it all. "Which one do you want your loved one in?" he asked.

None of them, I wanted to scream. But I didn't. Instead, with considerable reserve, I helped mother and my sister make a moderately priced choice, sign some papers, write an obituary, and choose a time and place for the service.

After making these arrangements, Bill and I got back on a plane and flew to Chicago for a sold-out concert at McCormick Place. We did not mention the events of our day to the audience, but tried to give the concert they anticipated. At the end of the first half, we started our "usual" song before intermission. As Danny, Bill's brother and the third member of our trio, sang the last verse, it was as if I had never heard it before, much less written the words myself:

And then one day I'll cross death's river;
I'll fight life's final war with pain —
And then as faith gives way to victory,
I'll see the lights of glory and I'll know He reigns.

Because He lives, I can face tomorrow.

The truth of the Resurrection warmed the frozen edges of my soul, and the seeds of hope that had been buried under the chill of death quickened in my spirit. It was as if I could hear my father saying, as I had so often heard him from the pulpit, "to be absent from the body is to be present with the Lord." And I knew that death had been dealt a fatal blow by my risen Lord. Death had no sting; *we could face tomorrow.*

Over the years this song has returned to reassure us that this is the central truth of life. Because He lives, we can face tomorrow. Many times since then, as our children grew, our business life changed, our fortunes shifted, or our direction clouded, our family has found assurance in this very personal song, "our song." It has been a joy and somewhat of a surprise that this song, so personal to us, has been so meaningful to others.

This has been the song we've held to as our promise from God for the precious lives entrusted to us. When Benjamin was in the turbulent adolescent years and felt confused by life, we often found ourselves saying, "Just hang on, Son; we'll get through this. The song that has been the most meaningful to people across the country is your song. It is God's promise to you; He is making you into a man of God."

"Because He Lives" has been our family's song — for living. And when we have said good-bye to close loved ones, it has been our song — our song for dying. The Resurrection is the truth that brings victory and hope. Life wins! Life wins!

God Gave the Song

You ask me why my heart keeps singing,
Why I can sing when things go wrong;
But since I've found the source of music,
I just can't help it, God gave the song.

Come walk with me thru fields and forests;
We'll climb the hills and still hear that song,
For even hills resound with music —
They just can't help it. God gave the song.

Yes, God gave the song. It's always been with us.
The song came into our world through a manger — a manger in
  Bethlehem.
It was a simple song — a simple lovely song for every man.
Right from the first, some tried to ignore it. They said,
"There's no song! It simply doesn't exist."

Others just tried to change the tune. They made laws to stop it.
Armies marched against it. They killed some who sang the song.
They screamed at it in fury, they tried to drown it out.
Finally they nailed that song to a tree.
They said to themselves, "There . . . that should take care of that!"
But it didn't!

What's that I hear? I still hear that music!
Day after day, that song goes on.
For once you know that source of music,
You'll always hear it, God gave the song.

Come on and join! It's the song of Jesus.
Day after day, that song goes on.
For once you know the source of music,
You'll always hear it, God gave the song.

God Gave the Song

Both Bill and I began our careers teaching English in high school. Even though we ended up creating work that is in some way connected with music, writing has been our life. Because of this, we have come in contact with many aspiring writers — young and old — who want the magic formula for successful writing. Is there a certain routine? What are the methods and the formulas writers use? How do writers analyze the market and the audience?

Our answer is a simple one. If you don't feel as if you'll choke to death if you don't write, you're probably not a writer. A person with a passion to write can study the forms, sharpen the skills, and practice the use of figures of speech. He or she can learn to recognize and use rhyme schemes, meters, and literary devices. All that may be useful, but ultimately writers write because they have no choice. Even if no one ever read or praised or bought her writing, a writer would have to write.

I love Madeleine L'Engle's statement, in her book *Walking on Water,* that "art is incarnational." For a writer a seed of truth lodges somewhere in the soul, and she or he can't stop its growth any more than a mother can stop the growth of the child she has conceived, unless it is aborted. It must be — it will be — delivered to the world. And the writing of a thing is just the beginning. Like a baby, if it is to survive, it must be shaped and disciplined and nurtured to maturity. It may then be accepted or rejected, but the writer has delivered it full-blown into the world. That is the writer's job; that is the writer's passion.

Sometimes secular interviewers ask us how we can keep writing songs about religious themes. After more than six hundred songs, wouldn't we run out of ideas? Wouldn't we get bored with the Jesus theme? To those questions we can only answer that it is no more possible to exhaust the story of Jesus than it is to run out of stories of life itself. The story, like the steadfast love of the Lord, is new every morning.

The Song of Life has to be written; there is no better and no other explanation than that. The song dictates its own time and place. It chooses its own circumstances. It grows in daily experience until it just can't stay inside any longer. The writer gets uncomfortable, pregnant with the growing life. It can't be stopped!

It might be after breakfast some morning; it might be late at night. It could be on a tour bus or on an airplane at thirty thousand feet. It could be at the grocery store or at a cabin in the woods. It could be on vacation or on the way to pick up the kids from school. When it's time, a song will come.

Some songs take a midwife. Some require long labor. Other songs pour out so unexpectedly that you are completely unprepared. You grab whatever instruments are handy: a napkin in a restaurant, a canceled check, a used envelope, the sole of your shoe — a piece of chalk, a stub of a pencil.

But the option to say, "Oh, I don't think so. I've decided not to deliver this," is just not available to an inspired writer. A writer writes. Like a fish swims or a bird flies or a living being breathes.

Stop the song? The song can no more be stopped than the passage of the seasons. In God's own time the song will sing itself into the world.

Why and how do we write a song?

We just can't help it. That's all.

He Touched Me

Shackled by a heavy burden,
'Neath a load of guilt and shame —
Then the hand of Jesus touched me,
And now I am no longer the same!

He touched me
Oh, He touched me!
And oh, the joy that floods my soul!
Something happened and now I know,
He touched me
And made me whole.

Since I met this blessed Savior,
Since He cleansed and made me whole,
I will never cease to praise Him;
I'll shout it while eternity rolls!

He Touched Me

When we were first married we were both teaching high school. (Bill was teaching English, and I was teaching English and French.) On the weekends Bill was directing the music program at a local church. We were beginning to write songs to fill the voids we perceived in expression, often in response to a sermon or prayer or something learned from Scripture and our own lives. We would say, "There ought to be a song that says. . ." And then we would write one. We'd mimeograph (remember those machines?) the handwritten copies and then try them out on the choir at Wednesday night rehearsal. If they liked the song, we admitted that we'd written it. If they didn't, we kept our mouths shut, and that would be the end of that song.

About this same time Doug Oldham began attending our church. We knew Doug and his family. His father, Dale, had formerly pastored the large Park Place Church near Anderson College and had been the voice of the Christian Brotherhood Hour, the national radio broadcast of the Church of God. Doug had been a part of his father's ministry and of several other ministries, including that of Cadel Tabernacle in Indianapolis.

But Doug's life had fallen apart; his wife Laura had taken the children and left; the popularity he once enjoyed had changed to loneliness and despair. At one point Doug was so desperate and depressed that he had taken a loaded revolver and driven around trying to get the nerve to kill himself. As he drove he was aware enough of the presence of the Lord to cry out loud to this God he thought he'd left behind, "If You're there, either give me something worth living for or the guts to pull this trigger."

He did not end his life that day, but instead began the process of letting God put the broken pieces of his life back together. Doug admitted that what was wrong was not the fault of his parents or the church or his wife, but it was a result of his own selfish choices. He realized how he'd hurt the ones who loved him most and asked God for forgiveness. Then he tried to reestablish the broken lines of communication so he could ask forgiveness of those whose lives he'd torn apart.

The changes were not immediate, but as Doug learned to be honest with God and himself, the Great Physician was able to heal Doug from the inside out. Little by little Doug traded a lifetime of bad habits for bits of wholeness.

This is the man who began to slip into the back pew of South Meridian Church in Anderson where Bill was serving as minister of music. Most of us look back over our lives and see that the most painful times are also the times of greatest growth and discovery. Eventually and gradually, with a lot of prayer and efforts at communication, Doug and Laura put their home back together and rebuilt a fragile but growing trust. Sometimes Laura doubted that what they had left to work with was enough to mend such a fractured relationship. She wrote this about those fears:

> One day several months down the road, I had a real attack of anxiety over whether I could ever really trust Doug again. The enemy of our souls can really work on a woman's imagination and he had me in his grip.
>
> I went to the bedroom, got down on my knees, and prayed for help, "Help me to trust and get rid of this gnawing fear." A bit of Scripture kept coming persistently to mind. I got up, found a Bible, and looked it up in Matthew. The phrase I kept hearing was, "The one whom you feared is dead." The Scripture refers to Herod. An angel appeared to Joseph in a dream saying, "Take the child and Mary and go back to your home. The one who sought the child's life is dead." [See Matthew 2:20.] The Lord was very plainly saying to me, "The Doug you feared is dead. Take the children and go home," which I had done. When the Lord saves a man and changes him, the old one is dead. Now the task for me was to believe it.

Not only did Laura need assurance from God, their three little girls had to learn to live without fear and to relate to the new Doug, who was becoming a real father.

To begin again, Doug and Laura even sold their old house and bought a new one that held no bad memories. On one visit to the old house to retrieve belongings, Doug's daughter ran and hid behind the door as she had many times before when she'd heard her daddy coming. Seeing this, Doug went to his child and stooped down to talk to her. "Honey, you don't have to be afraid. You've got a new Daddy now," he whispered. "Thanks to Calvary, we don't live here anymore."

A few days later, when Doug and Laura told Bill and me that story, we were inspired to write the song Doug was to sing for years afterward. It was and has continued to be Doug's song:

> *Thanks to Calv'ry I am not the man I used to be —*
> *Thanks to Calv'ry things are different than before —*
> *While the tears ran down my face, I tried to tell them*
> *"Thanks to Calv'ry I don't come here anymore."*

As Doug continued to put his life together, he knew he needed to restore his relationship with his father, Dale. God worked there as well. Dale and Bill wrote "Something Worth Living For" about Doug's desperate prayer that night in the car. Before long Dale asked Doug to go with him and sing — and tell what God was doing in his marriage — at a series of revivals Dale had scheduled. Doug in turn asked if Bill would play piano for the services and for Doug. Doug was singing many of the new songs Bill and I had written, such as "Lovest Thou Me?" "In the Upper Room," "Have You Had a Gethsemane?" "Something Worth Living For," and Bill's earlier song "I've Been to Calvary," which had been recorded by the Speer Family. Bill and I decided that agreeing to play for Doug would help Doug — and our songs.

After one of those services, on a Saturday night in Huntington, Indiana, Bill called me to say that God was truly up to something in the meeting and in Doug. The spirit of the meeting had been unusually warm and sweet. The Oldhams had noticed the same thing and, driving home that night, the three men talked about what had happened in the service, how people were so visibly touched and changed by the Spirit.

"Bill," Dr. Dale said, "there's something about the word *touch*. To think that the awesome God could touch our lives is a wonderful thing. You should write a song that says, 'He touched me; oh, He touched me.'"

The next morning, before church, Bill played on the piano the melody that had been going through his head all night. I heard him singing, "He touched me; Oh, He touched me, and oh, the joy that floods my soul. . . ." It was a beautiful, simple melody with passion and emotion.

Soon Bill called me to come into the little back room where we had the piano in the small house we'd rented from Bill's parents. He had scribbled down the lyrics to two verses and a chorus. "See what you think," he said, singing through what he'd written:

Shackled by a heavy burden,
'Neath a load of guilt and shame —
Then the hand of Jesus touched me,
And now I am no longer the same!

I suggested he change the line "Now I am no longer the same." "It could be stronger, I think; more specific," I said.

He acknowledged my suggestion, then went on to sing the second verse. I thought that verse was good as it was — direct and innocent, filled with gratitude, as we really are when we become new in Christ

Jesus — children again — yet aware of where we've been. Fortunately, Bill did not take my advice about the last line of the first verse. He kept it as it was. In fact, nothing changed. The whole song remained exactly as it first came to him.

Later that very day, Bill called Doug and sang it for him. By the next weekend Doug was performing it. It was his story. It was our story. And it has turned out to be everybody's story. The line I had objected to has probably been the secret to the song's great success, because each of us is able to read our own specific circumstances into that line: No matter what we've been, when we are touched by God we can honestly say, "Now I'm no longer the same!"

Doug was the first person to record "He Touched Me" as well as "Something Worth Living For" and "Thanks to Calvary (I Don't Live Here Anymore)." He sang them all over the country as God continued the work of restoring his life and his family.

"He Touched Me" has been recorded more than any other song we have written — by artists such as the Imperials, George Beverly Shea, Kate Smith, Jimmy Durante, and Elvis Presley. It has been translated into dozens of languages and sung around the world. Bill still likes to remind me that this is one song he wrote all by himself, and I still cringe a little when I think that we could have lost its most powerful line . . . had he listened to me.

I Believe in a Hill Called Mount Calvary

There are things as we travel this earth's shifting sands
That transcend all the reason of man,
But the things that matter the most in this world —
They can never be held in our hand.

> I believe in a hill called Mount Calvary
> I'll believe whatever the cost
> And when time has surrendered and earth is no more,
> I'll still cling to that old rugged cross.

I believe that the Christ who was slain on the cross
Has the power to change lives today,
For He changed me completely — a new life is mine!
That is why by the cross I will stay.

I believe that this life with its great mysteries
Surely someday will come to an end;
But faith will conquer the darkness and death
And will lead me at last to my Friend.

> I believe in a hill called Mount Calvary
> I'll believe whatever the cost
> And when time has surrendered and earth is no more,
> I'll still cling to that old rugged cross.

I Believe in a Hill Called Mount Calvary

"But how do you explain an omnipotent God letting bad things happen to good people?"

"Is God sovereign? If so, are we robots? Do we have any choices or are we predestined to choose what we choose? . . . So why witness, send missionaries, minister?"

"If God knows what we need more than we do, if He knows our thoughts and desires, if He sees the future and charts our path, why pray? Why not just wait for Him to do whatever He's going to do anyway?"

The questions seem to fly as soon as we confess a faith in Jesus Christ, as if finding a question not yet fully answered gives the questioner some ground to stand on for not believing.

And perhaps for all of us there is a time in our young lives when we feel we have the luxury of always questioning and never resolving the great issues of life. But sooner or later inquisitors and critics choose to resolve some major questions, or they become cynics.

For many, the time for deciding comes as we birth a new generation. It's one thing to sit around in college dormitories discussing the unsolvable problems of the universe. It's another to hold your own newborn baby in your arms and realize that what this child thinks and feels and believes will be largely your responsibility. You realize you will never have all the answers to all the questions, but you also know there are at least a few things you'd better get nailed down. Turbulent spirits must lay a few things to rest, and although we can't know everything, we begin to realize we must know a few things for sure. Jesus taught that the evidence that confirms our leaps of faith comes after we risk believing, not before.

Bill and I wrote "I Believe in a Hill Called Mount Calvary" at a fork in the road for our lives. We hadn't then, nor have we now, resolved all the questions. But we chose to risk everything we were or ever hoped to be on a few things that began for us a growing relationship with Christ.

We, like most human beings, would have preferred that God prove Himself before we risked believing. None of us wants to make a fool of himself. "If You prove You're real, I'll believe" is the way most of us approach the omniscient Jehovah. But God is not an axiom of science. He is the great I Am, and it is not He but each of us who is on trial. Judas (not Iscariot) tried the "play it safe" avenue of reasoning with Jesus. "Reveal Yourself to the world at large. It would be so much easier, then, to make people believe in You. These miracles are great! Could you take this show on the road?" But Jesus' answer was quick. "I will only reveal myself to those who love me." (See John 14:22–24 LB.)

Bill and I had to learn that God required that we first risk, believe, love. The "knowing" results then, only from relationship. And relationship — not evidence or knowledge or miracles or "gifts" — had to be our passion. What we considered the process, God considers the goal. Once we dared to risk believing, all the tough circumstances of life would then crowd us to Christ, shove us closer to Him, nudge us into dependency on Him. That — *relationship* — is His goal. "I will only reveal myself to those who love me and obey me," Jesus said.

Some years ago a slogan made its way to bumper stickers and lapel pins. I'm sure it was well intended, but I never really liked the phrase — "TRY JESUS." It reminded me of a tray of hors d'oeuvres at a party. If you don't like the shrimp canapés, try the bacon-wrapped mini-hotdogs or the tiny cheese tarts.

But we have found that serving Jesus is not a taste sampling. It's not a risk-free bet. It's not a for-profit investment, an "if you want to get, then you have to give" deal. It's a leap into the unknown, risking everything you have and are on the Way beyond proof, not for financial gain, not for good feelings, not to get "gifts" — even gifts of the Spirit, though all of those things may result from this choice somewhere down the road.

If they do, chances are we will be the last to know. Most likely we will feel very inadequate and ordinary when we hear someone else say, "She is one of the most patient people I know," or "He is a kind and gentle man of integrity." *Who me?* may be our quick response.

That is how we come to know that in pursuit of a relationship with Jesus, we are being changed into His likeness. At that point, all the bewildering questions may remain unanswered. But — as the old-timers used to say — we are finding we don't have such a gnawing need to know the answers when we know the Answer. We are coming, as the poet Rilke said, to love the question and to get more comfortable with the paradox of God. When we trust the author, we don't have to know the story. We just know it will be true.

We Americans have lived primarily in a country friendly to the Gospel. Oh, we may have what we consider "persecution" in some of our homes or we may work in an "unfriendly" environment. But we have not known persecution as Paul knew it or a world in which Christians are beheaded, burned at the stake, or thrown to the lions.

But history has shown that the winds of public opinion are fickle. Our freedom to worship openly, form Bible study groups in our homes, hold Christian concerts in public arenas, praise God with sixty thousand Promise Keepers, declare we are "women of faith" with thousands of other believers, could be replaced by regulations, repression, or even imprisonment.

Only "relationship" would stand through such a change. If we serve God because we think "serving Jesus really pays" in a material sense, we would likely be blown away like chaff on a threshing floor. If we're hanging around the church because we like fellowships and enjoy the warm feelings of "the womb," we would most certainly be torn away like helpless children in wartime.

Only a growing relationship with the living God, bought by the blood of His Son Jesus, sustained by the nurturing of His Holy Spirit internally, will endure.

When Corrie ten Boom spoke at a Praise Gathering in her later years, she recounted a conversation she had as an adolescent with her father about the martyrs killed for the cause of Christ. She told her father she didn't think she'd be capable of standing firm if she were tortured for her faith or her family were killed before her eyes. In short, she didn't think she could be a martyr.

Her father gave an insightful answer, asking her a question: "When our family took that train trip, when did I give you children your tickets?"

"Why, just when it was time to get on the train," she answered.

"If God asks you to give your life for His sake, He'll give you the grace to do it when the time comes."

Little did she know then that she'd be the only one of her family to survive the atrocities of Nazi prison camps, where they'd been sent for their compassionate role in harboring Jews and helping them to escape.

Even as an octogenarian Corrie would quickly have said she hadn't answered all the theological questions people often use as an obstacle to faith, but she loved to sing a song based on the apostle Paul's testimony:

But I know whom I have believed
And am persuaded that He is able
To keep that which I've committed
Unto Him against that day!

Going Home

Many times in my childhood
When we'd travel so far,
By nightfall how weary I'd grow;
Father's arm would slip 'round me,
So gently he'd say,
"My child, we're going home."

Now the twilight is fading
And the day soon shall end;
I get homesick the farther I roam,
But my Father has led me
Each step of the way,
And now we're going home.

Going home, I'm going home —
There's nothing to hold me here;
I've caught a glimpse of that heav'nly land,
Praise God, I'm going home.

Oh my heart gets so heavy
And I'm longing to see
My loved ones and friends I have known;
Ev'ry step draws me nearer
To the land of my dreams;
Praise God, I'm going home.

Going home, I'm going home,
There's nothing to hold me here;
I've caught a glimpse of that heav'nly land.
Praise God, I'm going home!

Going Home

Bill and I had been away from home about a week, holding services in a church in eastern Tennessee. Our little Suzanne had been as patient as a one-year-old could be. Finally the last night, we said good-bye to our friends and packed our bags and boxes into our station wagon. I shook hands with the last of the people in the church lobby, then headed for the Sunday school room we had used as a dressing room — to put Suzanne's pajamas on her and jump into my jeans for the long drive home from Tennessee to Indiana.

As we pulled out of the parking lot, Suzanne asked, "Where are we going now, Mommy?" Children of traveling parents ask that question a lot.

"Home, Sweetheart," Bill answered. "We're going home."

She clapped her hands and made up a song. "Going home. We're going home," she sang until she finally fell asleep.

As we drove away from the city lights and onto the highway, I remembered as a child how safe it felt in the warm cocoon of our family car — heading home. My parents traveled often to conventions and other ministerial meetings. We were gone so often that my mother bought me an extra set of schoolbooks so I could keep up my work. There was something so comforting about finally leaving the place we'd been visiting to head home where we belonged.

Bill must have been thinking about something very similar.

"I remember when I was a kid, Mom and Dad would take us to Nashville to the Ryman Auditorium for the 'all-night singings,'" he mused. "I'd beg and beg until Dad would finally agree to make the trip. He'd say, 'We'll go, but you better stay in that seat for every bit of that singing.'

"I think he was sorry he ever said that when, at one in the morning, I was still there listening to the very last song! And yet I remember how happy I felt when Dad would put his arm around my shoulder and say, 'Come on; let's go home,' and we'd pile in the car and head for home. I was so full of music and dreams about someday singing like that that I wouldn't stop talking for miles."

Suzanne had given us an idea for a new song, and her little tune kept going through our minds. Children who have to travel as much as ours did seldom beg to go someplace. Instead, they beg to stay home. Home is the sweetest place of all. They know; they've been everywhere else!

In a way we're all children of a traveling family. We've seen some nice places. We've stayed in some nice houses. We've had some memorable experiences and met some great people. But we really don't live there.

And sometimes the miles get long and the attractions — no matter how exciting — get to be just another county fair. No matter how much we sleep, we don't ever seem to be at rest. No matter how sweet the fellowship or how pleasant the hospitality, we don't ever seem to really "belong."

But one of these days our Father will scoop us up in His strong arms and we will hear Him say those sweet and comforting words, "Come on, child. We're going home."

Since Jesus Passed By

Like the blind man I wandered,
So lost and undone,
A beggar so helpless,
Without God or His Son;
Then my Savior in mercy,
Heard and answered my cry — and
Oh, what a diff'rence since Jesus passed by!

Since Jesus passed by,
Since Jesus passed by,
Oh, what a diff'rence since Jesus passed by!
Well, I can't explain it,
And I cannot tell you why — but
Oh, what a diff'rence,
Since Jesus passed by!

All my yesterdays are buried in the deepest of the sea;
That old load of guilt I carried
Is all gone. Praise God, I'm free!
Looking for that bright tomorrow,
Where no tears will dim the eye —
Oh, what a diff'rence since Jesus passed by!

Since Jesus passed by,
Since Jesus passed by,
Oh, what a diff'rence since Jesus passed by!
Well, I can't explain it,
And I cannot tell you why, — but
Oh, what a diff'rence since Jesus passed by!

Since Jesus Passed By

One morning while Bill was gone to speak at a choral workshop, I stayed behind in our hotel in Norfolk, Virginia. I was busy writing in our room on the sixth floor when the sound of a marching band drew me to a window. Below me in the street I saw a most colorful homecoming parade passing by! Floats of every color and description proclaimed that education was SERVING TODAY — BUILDING TOMORROW! Energetic bands gave enthusiastic endorsement to the statement. Children, parents, high school students, and alumni lined the streets, waving to parade participants who waved back from the floats. Now and again I caught sight of parents who had spotted their one most important parader. Parents waved excitedly and ran along the curb, camera in hand, trying to keep that special son or daughter in sight.

Just across the street a row of preschoolers in pink romper suits and furry jackets lined the curb; the parade must have seemed like a wonderland of color and sounds to them. I caught the contagion of their excitement as they tapped their heels to the rhythms and clapped their tiny hands.

Confetti drifted in green and yellow clouds on the crisp October breezes. I watched mounds of popcorn and paper cupfuls of cider disappear, completing the total sensory experience. I love a parade!

When Bill returned, only silent clues of the parade remained: scattered bits of confetti, empty paper cups and popcorn boxes, petals from chrysanthemum pom-poms, a few tattered crepe paper streamers from the floats, a broken lawn chair or two. "What's all that about down there?" Bill asked. "Why is the street so littered?"

"A homecoming parade went by this morning. You should have been here."

In contrast to that parade image in my mind is a scene Bill and I saw in a small town in our area. A few years back on Palm Sunday, a terrible tornado ravaged central Indiana. Whole villages were practically wiped out. Trailer parks were smashed and broken. Bill and I drove along the tornado's route. It was so disheartening to see the storekeepers standing outside their destroyed businesses, trying to assess the damage. One brand-new subdivision of brick homes was almost flattened.

But for us it was even sadder to see what had happened to the countryside. Mature forests were uprooted, giant trees twisted like little twigs. Crops carefully planted and nurtured were flooded and flattened. And those big, old two-story Indiana farm homes that had been handed down from generation to generation — destroyed. We passed one such farmhouse, and all that was left was the hearth. One could almost hear the voices of the children that house had sheltered, the families that had gathered after a hard day in the fields to sit by the fireplace and share a warm supper. Now on the rubble stood a man and woman about seventy years old. She wore a print apron and he, worn denim overalls. As they looked at what had been a lifetime of hard work, they wept like little children.

We passed another farmhouse, all swept away except for the framework. Even the furniture and appliances were blown about the yard and broken. Some friends riding with us said this family — with small children — had been killed. Just before we drove away, we noticed something we've never been able to forget. Slung over a second-story rafter was a young girl's doll — a gruesome reminder of what had happened at that place. As we continued on down the highway, I couldn't get that sight out of my mind — that doll — that symbol of the tragedy of it all.

Then I began to wonder what it would have been like to walk down a street where Jesus had walked. Maybe you'd never met this man Jesus, never heard His name. But as you walk down the cobblestone street, you can tell that something has happened here. At the side of the road lies a broken crutch that someone has thrown high in the air and let bound to the pavement, never to be retrieved! You walk on a little farther and see a pile of dirty, rotten, stinking bandages that some leper has torn away — when he looked and found his skin clean and new as a child's. On down the street there is a mattress on which some friends had carried a paralyzed man, but it's abandoned because the man walked his way home.

You see all these things, but you don't quite understand. You notice a man at the end of the street, and you decide to ask him what it all means. You rush up to him, intending to ask, but something about him makes you stop. Here is a grown man, holding a delicate rose. The way he's holding it — gently, almost worshipfully — is odd. And when you see his face, the look in his eyes, the tears streaming down his cheeks, it dawns on you that this man is seeing a rose for the very first time! Out of respect you stand still for a moment and then, when you dare, you touch him on the arm and ask, "Mister, what happened here? What does all this mean?" He looks up at you with eyes as wide open as he can get them, and he says, "Oh, friend, weren't you here? Haven't you heard? Jesus passed by! Jesus passed by! You see, I was born blind. Had no hope of ever seeing, and this man they call Jesus passed by this very road, and He touched my eyes, as He touched so many others. Oh, I wish you could have been here!"

The man can't stay to talk longer. Still holding the rose in his hands, he runs down the street calling for his friends. "John! Matthew! Come look at me! Jesus passed by!" And he calls to his wife and says, "Mary, Mary, come here — and bring me the babies! Oh, Mary, I've held them on my lap, and I've touched their little faces with my hands, but I've never seen what they look like. Mary, things are going to be different. So different. Jesus passed by! Jesus passed by. . . ."

We weren't there that day on that road, but Bill and I have been on many a "street" where Jesus has passed by, and everywhere He walks, He leaves behind a trail of wholeness and completeness and joy that is unmistakably His touch.

When it comes right down to it, that is why we are believers. Theology is an interesting school of thought. The Bible is beautiful literature. Sitting in a quiet sanctuary, bathed in the amber light from stained-glass windows, having our jangled nerves soothed by the chords from an organ — all that is inspiring. But to tell you the truth, when we leave the classroom, close the church door, and walk out into the real world, it is the indisputable proof of changed lives that makes us believers.

The Longer I Serve Him
(The Sweeter He Grows)

Since I started for the kingdom,
Since my life He controls,
Since I gave my heart to Jesus,
THE LONGER I SERVE HIM, the sweeter He grows.

THE LONGER I SERVE HIM, the sweeter He grows;
The more that I love Him, more love He bestows.
Each day is like heaven; my heart overflows,
THE LONGER I SERVE HIM, the sweeter He grows.

Ev'ry need He is supplying;
Plenteous grace He bestows,
Ev'ry day my way gets brighter —
THE LONGER I SERVE HIM, the sweeter He grows.

The Longer I Serve Him

We called her "Mom" Hartwell partly because she was Bill's grandmother and partly because she was everybody's "Mom."

She had raised seven children of her own, a couple of her grandchildren, and several other children. And it was well known around the Innesdale neighborhood of Alexandria, Indiana, that anyone else who needed a warm meal or a place to stay would always be welcomed at the Hartwell house. Even stray dogs and cats knew where they could get something to eat and probably a permanent home if they behaved themselves.

I loved her from the start. She was Irish like my own grandmother and, like her, she baked great bread and berry pies, grew flowers everywhere, and had an orchard and a huge garden full of summer fruits and vegetables, which she canned in scalded Ball jars as the crops ripened.

She read and wrote poetry, played hymns on an old upright piano, and loved to talk about Jesus.

When Bill first took me to Mom Hartwell's house, I felt as if I had come home to someone I'd lost at age fourteen, when my own dear grandmother had died. I knew this woman.

She took me in without a question. If Billy Jim loved me, that was enough for her. She tied an apron around my middle, handed me a stack of unmatched plates tall enough to set a banquet hall, and pointed me toward the long table in what served as a dining room in this well-worn house. With that gesture, I was "family" and I remained so.

There were many dinners after that first one. Kids of all sizes and shapes would swarm through the house, letting the screen door slam behind them as they moved toward Mom's kitchen stove, like metal shavings drawn to a magnet. They'd lift the lids off simmering pots of fresh green beans or steaming mashed potatoes, bubbling kettles of boiling corn on the cob, hot roasters full of baked chickens.

I would join the brigades of granddaughters, nieces, cousins, and daughters-in-law who served up the garden vegetables, starches, and meats into huge white serving dishes, poured gallons of iced tea and lemonade, and filled huge crockery mugs with strong hot coffee from the graniteware coffeepot that always simmered on the back of the stove.

By the time dinner was on the table, the men would have made their way into the house from the yard, where they'd been standing around with thumbs in their back pockets, talking in little clumps about the weather and the crops and the price of Angus cattle.

Half Native-American, Pop would tower above the other men, his bald head a full shade lighter than the brown suntanned skin of his face and neck. His big gruff voice would boom out at the children scurrying like mice among grown-up legs. "Get quiet, kids!" Then in a gentler tone, "Mom, pray."

And in her soft Irish tones Mom Hartwell would "approach the throne of God," and she stayed there until all the kids had been prayed for, the families had been lifted up, and the meats and vegetables had been blessed to the good of our bodies, and our bodies to the service of the Lord.

Then a happy roar would rise to fill the tiny house as the feast was consumed to the recitations of great memories, the telling of funny stories, and peals of uproarious laughter.

Like a sponge tossed up on the shore and dried out by the sun, I'd let this family's sweet tides of love wash over me. I was away from my own family, and my grandparents were gone. I'd think about how often Bill's family — now mine — had clung to the edge of poverty, raising food because they had to. I'd think about the old house, barely adequate to shelter such a huge crowd, mortgaged time and time again to keep the doors open to the little white frame church next door and to support a preacher there who also knew hard times.

I'd think about Pop, orphaned as a child and working odd jobs until he learned to farm and dig wells — how he lived out the truth that any honest work is "honorable work," as he'd say.

I'd think about Mom as the brown-eyed girl in the picture that hung in the front room. That small, pretty girl married big Burl Hartwell, who had no family, and together they started a family of their own. I'd heard her tell, still choking back the tears after all these years, how they had "lost" three babies — to pneumonia and diphtheria and "the croup" — in the days before antibiotics and emergency room medical care. I'd watched how she treasured the ones who lived, and how she couldn't "turn out any kid who needed a home."

In time Bill and I brought our first baby to this tiny house. Oh, but Mom was proud of that baby! She held her in the old maple rocker and sang to her the old hymns she'd come to love because she'd proven them true.

> *What a fellowship, what a joy divine;*
> *Leaning on the everlasting arms;*
> *What a blessedness! What a peace is mine!*
> *Leaning on the everlasting arms.*

"Play something, Billy Jim," she'd say as she held our baby. Bill would go to the old out-of-tune piano and play our newest song.

"Do you like this, Mom?" he'd ask, and then begin, "Shackled by a heavy burden..."

"Oh, my, that's beautiful, kids," she'd say.

I'd pray that moments like these would sink into the being of our baby girl, that her mind and soul would be schooled in the eternity of such precious times. Bill and I knew these were bonus days. For our baby to have her great-grandparents was a precious, fragile gift.

We lost Pop first. Maybe that was a good thing, because he could never have lived without Mom. And then she got sick. (It seems that people who love each other don't live long alone.) The seven children fought — not about who'd *have* to take care of her, but about who would *get* to take care of her.

We watched her slip from us. At times she'd be delirious, partly from the stroke and partly from the medication. We braced ourselves to accept a common pattern, where the conscious mind digs deep into the subconscious, dredging up morsels that are dark and uncharacteristic, shocking the family with ugly words and angry profanities. These occurrences can't be helped and no blame must be affixed to them.

But this didn't happen with Mom. As we sat by her bedside, she would sing in her delirium the old songs about her precious Jesus. "Oh, He is so precious to me," she'd sing. "Yes, He is so precious to me." Or sometimes she'd mumble words barely audible. We'd lean close to her lips, "Jesus," she'd whisper. "How good He is. Jesus."

One day toward the end, Mom was lucid and able to talk to us. We sat by her bed, Bill and I, with our baby girl, Suzanne. Mom loved to see the babies. She was recalling moments both rewarding and difficult. After a while Bill said, "Mom, you've lived a long time. We're just starting out with our baby and our lives. Tell me, has it been worth it, serving Jesus all these years?"

She looked at him with that Irish twinkle in her still snappy brown eyes. "Billy," she said, "the longer I serve Him, the sweeter He grows."

Not long after that, still forming the name of Jesus with her lips, she slipped out of our arms and into His. By then, the words she'd left us had shaped themselves into a song. It was published with the title "The Longer I Serve Him," but for Bill and me it will always be "The Last Will and Testament of Mom Hartwell." It was all she had to leave us, but we know we have inherited great wealth.

There's Something About That Name

Jesus. Jesus. Jesus. There's just something about that name.
Master, Savior, Jesus — Like the fragrance after the rain;
Jesus! Jesus! Jesus! Let all heaven and earth proclaim!
Kings and kingdoms will all pass away,
But there's something about that name.

Jesus. The mere mention of His name can calm the storm, heal the broken, raise the dead. At the name of Jesus, I've seen sin-hardened men melt, derelicts transformed, the lights of hope put back into the eyes of a hopeless child. . . .

At the name of Jesus, hatred and bitterness turn to love and forgiveness; arguments cease.

I've heard a mother softly breathe His name at the bedside of a child delirious from fever, and I've watched as that little body grew quiet and the fevered brow became cool.

I've sat beside a dying saint, her body racked with pain, who in those final fleeting seconds summoned her last ounce of ebbing strength to whisper earth's sweetest name — "Jesus, Jesus. . ."

Emperors have tried to destroy it; philosophies have tried to stamp it out. Tyrants have tried to wash it from the face of the earth with the very blood of those who claimed it. Yet still it stands.

And there shall be the final day when every voice that has ever uttered a sound — every voice of Adam's race — shall rise in one mighty chorus to proclaim the name of Jesus, for in that day "every knee shall bow and every tongue shall confess that Jesus Christ is Lord!!!"

So, you see, it was not mere chance that caused the angel one night long ago to say to a virgin maiden, "His name shall be called JESUS."

Jesus — Jesus — Jesus
There is something — something about that name. . . .

There's Something About That Name

W e used to sing a song at the end of some church services: "Jesus is all that I need." I never really liked that song much. I would argue in my mind whenever we sang it, *Well, I, for one, need a lot more. I need someone to love me; I need a warm body, a friendly face, someone to talk to at breakfast, and — more than that — someone who will talk back. I need quiet walks on the beach and a good cup of coffee with a friend to whom I don't have to explain myself.*

How shallow I was. Over the years I have come to notice that in the Gospel accounts, whenever someone had a need, Jesus answered with the ancient God words: "I am." And life is teaching me why Jesus answered with the words "I am."

I can hear His disciples. Around the campfire on the Sea of Galilee, they're singing the chorus, "Jesus is all that I need," and Peter says — in his typical blurt-it-right-out fashion — "Well, that's all well and good, but I for one need some supper!" And Jesus answers simply but with a certain finality, "*I am* the Bread."

There is the woman at the well. As she lifts to the surface the heavy bucket brimming with sweet water, she thinks, *How lovely to have this deep well that has survived all the generations. I may be an outcast, but at least I have this well. I need this water.* Suddenly the stranger who has just asked her for a drink says, "If only you knew, you'd ask Me for a drink. This well is temporary, but *I am* the Water that never runs dry, and I quench thirsts no water can satisfy."

Mary and Martha see Jesus coming down the dusty road to Bethany. They run to meet Him. Martha blurts out, "Our brother, Lazarus, is dead, and to tell you the truth, I just can't believe that You didn't come. What took You so long when You knew he was so sick? If You had been here, he would not have died!" Martha, so full of "what ifs." Jesus catches her by the shoulders and lifts her chin so that she can't avoid His eyes that are looking directly into hers. "*I am* the Resurrection and the Life," He says.

Bewildered by what is obviously a going-away party, Jesus' dearest friends begin to question. Where is He going? Can they come, too? How long will He be gone? Who's going to take His place as their teacher while He's gone? Oh, so many questions. "I will be gone a while, then you will come where I am," Jesus tells them, implying that there will be a space of distance or time or both when they will be separated and maybe disoriented. "How can we come to where You are?" asks Thomas. "We have no idea which way."

"*I am* the Way," He tells them.

"So!" shouts the hired harassers. "So, You are the King of the Jews!" Crude laughter bends them double in derision. "A King needs a scepter! Here!" screams a soldier, breaking off a reed from the tall weeds growing nearby. He jams the reed into Jesus' hands. The guards then grab Him by the ropes that bind those hands together and drag Him before Pilate, who joins in the mocking. "Let's paint a big sign: KING OF THE JEWS!" He stands back to size up his "art work," then turns to the Christ.

"So, are You the King?" Pilate asks, smirking at the ridiculous charade.

"*I am,*" is all He answers.

"So, what is the truth?" asks a cynical Pilate.

Even shackles and thorns and wounds and humiliation cannot throttle His authority: "*I am* the Truth."

And we, like them, come bringing our protests. The hungry Peter in us says, "But, we need someone to eat with, to share our deep hungers."

"*I am* the Bread," says Jesus, and we somehow know that He is addressing not just our growling stomachs, but our ravenous minds and shriveled spirits.

The cynical Pilate in us says, "We need intellectual stimulation. We need answers to the questions that will not be stilled. We hunger to learn. We have to ask. We want the truth."

"*I am* the Truth," we hear Him say to our questing minds.

Weary of being in charge of so many details and so many perplexities, we look around for someone to think for us. We're sick of "working out our own salvation"; this "fear and trembling" is getting wearisome. We need someone to do our thinking, maybe some charismatic leader who can make all the gray areas of our moral dilemmas black and white, give us some easy answers to these hard questions. Maybe a husband or authority to whom we must defer; maybe an evangelist or preacher — maybe a newly elected candidate to make some of these knotty social issues the government's problem instead of ours. We need a king; that's what we need, a monarch, a pro, a way-maker.

We look with horror at His disfigured body. Jesus straightens Himself — in spite of His agony — enough to look at us. He cannot reach for us. He is bound; He is powerless. Yet there is amazing power in His powerlessness. We see "King" emblazoned on His forehead. "For this purpose was I born, and for this cause came I into the world," is all he says before they lead Him away, carrying a heavy cross.

Frustrated, we wrap our dreams in grave clothes. Crying hot tears of grief, we set aside "what might have been." Yes, we agree with the poet, of all the words of tongue or pen, these are indeed the saddest.

Some who love us come to mourn the loss of our highest aspirations. Others appear to be mourners, but we know in reality they gloat, "Well, they've had more than their share. Now they know how we feel. We never even had a chance to dream."

We see Him coming and know His comfortable presence. We fling ourselves into His embrace. "Where were You?" we wail. "If You had been here … we needed Your presence but it's been so long. Why didn't You come to us? If You had been with us, our dreams would not have died!"

We feel His familiar, tender touch lifting our chin. Though we are blinded by hot tears, we cannot escape His eyes. "Daughter, Son, *I am* the Resurrection and the Life." And then we know He is peering into the frozen tomb of our soul; He calls in a loud voice, "My beloved, come forth!" We feel a stirring, a surge of life forcing its way through congealed veins. There is a warming that goes clear to our toes. At His voice, we, too, live!

The miles I have walked since I first resented that song "Jesus is all that I need" have taught me what I could have learned no other way: When Jesus is all you have, Jesus is, indeed, all you need. Two words: "*I am.*" They are all the words we ever need. They are the words that spoke worlds into existence. They are the words that God speaks into the void that is in each of us. They are the answer to all questions.

When a child is delirious with fever, listen for Jesus' "*I am,*" and know He is the cooling hand on her brow. When bitterness and grudges rip families apart and cause tender hearts to harden, "*I am*" is the power to heal and soften and restore trust. When the parents we love slip into eternity and we cannot call them back, we can be sure "*I am*" is the first welcoming voice they will hear on the other side. When tyrants threaten our planet and wipe out whole populations, "*I am*" are the words we can cling to for sanity in an insane world.

When from the ashes of bitter disappointment, new dreams rise like a phoenix on the strong wings of a new morning, and when we look back down the long road of our lives and see piles of ash like altars built along our path, we feel a simple chorus I once refused to sing rising in our hearts: "Jesus is all that I need."

He smiles at us — we know it — and whispers simply: *I am.*

Let's Just Praise the Lord

We'd like to thank you for your kindness; we thank you for your love;
We've been in heav'nly places, felt blessings from above;
We've been sharing all the good things the fam'ly can afford;
Let's just turn our praise t'ward heaven and praise the Lord.

Let's just praise the Lord! Praise the Lord!
Let's just lift our hands to heaven and praise the Lord!
Let's just praise the Lord, praise the Lord —
Let's just lift our hands t'ward heaven and praise the Lord!

Just the precious name of Jesus is worthy of our praise;
Let us bow our knees before Him, our hands to heaven raise.
When He comes in clouds of glory, with Him we'll ever reign;
We'll just lift our happy voices, and praise His name!

Let's just praise the Lord! Praise the Lord!
Let's just lift our hands to heaven and praise the Lord!
Let's just praise the Lord, praise the Lord —
Let's just lift our hands t'ward heaven and praise the Lord!

Let's Just Praise the Lord

*I*t was a concert on the East Coast. We had been warned that Easterners would be very reserved and not to expect much response from such a conservative audience. But much to our surprise, the people were warm and excited.

The audience was a multiethnic blend of believers with a wide range of ages. Right from the first song, they sang along enthusiastically and seemed to enjoy both the humor and the content as the concert progressed through the evening.

As we shared what God was teaching us and our young family, we felt a ready identity with our audience — people from many different backgrounds who had found Christ to be the answer for their families, too.

We sang "Because He Lives," "There's Something About That Name," and "The King Is Coming." At the end of the concert we were overwhelmed when the audience leaped to their feet and kept applauding. At first, it was gratifying to know they agreed with our message. But the applause continued until we felt uncomfortable with the response, which was no longer praising the Lord but being directed toward our group.

Finally Bill began to sing at the piano, "Oh, How I Love Jesus!" Gradually the audience stopped applauding and joined him. We could sense the praise turn again from being horizontally directed to us to being vertically directed to God, where it belonged.

That night after we got back to the bus, we talked about what had happened. "We need a song," Bill said, "that would thank people for being so kind and loving to us, but would help us all turn the praise heavenward, where it belongs."

"Why don't we just say exactly that?" I suggested.

So Bill turned to an electric keyboard we had on the bus, and I grabbed a yellow tablet and began to write:

> *We'd like to thank you for your kindness; thank you for your love,*
> *We've been in heavenly places, felt blessings from above.*
> *We've been sharing all the good things the family can afford,*
> *Let's just turn our praise toward heaven and praise the Lord.*

In the years since, we have been at times so full of gratitude and awe that we haven't been able to do anything else but sing "Let's just praise the Lord." At other times we haven't been able to see how God could possibly be there in the dark circumstances of life, yet we have learned that He was always — in all things — up to something good in our lives. That "good" is always eternal good, and we are learning that life is a process. To God process isn't a means to an end; it is the goal because His goal is to crowd us into a relationship with Him. Whatever sends us running to Him, makes us embrace Him, causes us to depend on Him, is the best good in our lives.

We once received a letter from a man criticizing this song and its use of the word *just*. "Why would you say 'just' praise the Lord?" he wrote. "Why not say, 'We always praise the Lord!' or 'We're happy to praise the Lord.'"

The same week we got a letter from a father who had backed out of his garage and run over his three-year-old son, playing on his tricycle behind the car. The despair over such a tragedy would have been unbearable had this man not been able to hold on to the hope that in all things God was at work in their family's lives for some eternal good. "Thank you for the song," he wrote. "I am discovering that we 'just' praise the Lord when there's nothing else we can do."

Some of life's circumstances seem senseless, and others, too painful to bear. But when we base our confidence on a perspective broader than this world's view, we can trust that what our sovereign God is working to accomplish is not the servant of this world's circumstances; rather, this world's circumstances are always being made the servant of His purposes.

Let's just praise the Lord!

Something Beautiful

If there ever were dreams
That were lofty and noble,
They were my dreams at the start;
And the hopes for life's best
Were the hopes that I harbored
Down deep in my heart;
But my dreams turned to ashes,
My castles all crumbled,
My fortune turned to loss,
So I wrapped it all
In the rags of my life,
And laid it at the cross!

Something beautiful, something good —
All my confusion He understood;
All I had to offer Him
Was brokenness and strife,
But He made something beautiful of my life.

Something Beautiful

*S*uzanne, our firstborn, was always the "project kid" around our
house. As long as we were making something, building something, painting something, cooking something, she was a contented
child. If I was washing dishes, she was standing on her little chair beside
me, her arms elbow-deep in dishwater, talking a mile a minute. If I was
making cookies, she was rolling dough and cutting it into thanksgiving
pumpkins, Valentine hearts, Easter bunnies, or stars of Bethlehem, then
sprinkling the shapes with colored sugar and silver pellets or smearing
the fresh-baked symbols with icing.

We had backyard circuses, Fourth of July patriot parades, neighborhood leaf-raking parties, pumpkin-carving competitions, and Easter
egg hunts. She enlisted cousins and friends in sidewalk art shows, a

summer craft gallery, and a town-sponsored fishing contest at our creek. Just give her a chain of projects from morning till night and she was a happy camper.

When she was almost three she was working one day with tempera paints at her little table in the corner of the family room. From the kitchen, out of the corner of my eye, I watched as she confidently made great strokes of strong colors across the large sheet of paper that covered the whole surface of her table. She kept dipping water and paint, as children love to do, when — on one trip from paint to paper — a big black blob dropped from her wet brush right into the middle of her picture. I watched her consider it, then try to make something that seemed intentional out of the blob. But because her paper was so soaked with too much, too wet paint, the black paint just spread out in little rivulets in all directions, invading the lovely yellows, reds, and greens.

Soon I heard her feet pattering across the living room to the bathroom. She came back with a washcloth and tried to soak up some of the paint, rubbing the soggy paper with the end of the cloth. By then she had rubbed a hole in the center of her picture, and the colors around it had turned an ugly umber.

It wasn't long before she was in tears. She picked up the drippy mess and brought it into the kitchen where I was working.

"Oh, Mommy," she sobbed, "I tried to make you something beautiful but just look! I dropped some paint." She heaved and caught her breath. "I tried to fix it, but it just got worse and now just look!"

I took the soggy painting and laid it on the counter, then knelt down beside her, took her in my arms and let her cry out her anguish and disappointment. Finally, when she was spent and could hear me, I said, "I think there is one more big piece of paper in the craft closet. Let me check."

I went to where we kept supplies and, sure enough, there was a clean sheet left. You should have seen her face when she took the paper and skipped off to her table to begin again!

So often we are like Suzanne and her painting. We start out with noble dreams and aspirations. We harbor high hopes and lofty ambitions. We make up our minds not to make the mistakes our parents made, not to choose the paths our sister chose, not to mess up like our brother did.

And at first we seem to be in control of our lives. We determine to create our own healthy environment. We decide never again to be the victim of other people's choices. But somehow, as Robert Frost said, "way leads on to way," and before we know it, we have passed our thirtieth birthday and life is getting complicated. By forty we are beginning to realize that we've made some choices we regret, taken some turns we never thought we'd take. Oh, we try to fix it on our own, to cover what our heart is telling us, but if the truth were known, we get up in the morning with a hole in our souls big enough to drive a Mack truck through. And in our rare honest moments we know we're no closer to our hopes and dreams than we were at the start.

Perhaps the best thing that can happen to us is to realize that we are not self-sufficient. Like a child we can take the mess we've made of things to a heavenly Father and say, "O Lord, I wanted so to make something beautiful of my life, but just look..."

The amazing thing about Jesus is that He doesn't just patch up our lives. He doesn't just "make do" out of what we have left. He gives us a brand-new sheet, a clean slate to start over, all new. This miracle called "grace" is this: No matter when we realize we've made shabby gods and give control to Him, He makes us new creations. With God, it's never "Plan B" or "second best." It's always "Plan A." And, if we let Him, He'll make something beautiful of *our* lives.

The Family of God

You will notice we say "brother" and "sister" 'round here;
It's because we're a family and these folks are so near.
When one has a heartache we all share the tears,
And rejoice in each vict'ry in this fam'ly so dear.

> I'm so glad I'm a part of the fam'ly of God!
> I've been washed in the fountain,
> Cleansed by His blood.
> Joint heirs with Jesus as we travel this sod,
> For I'm part of the fam'ly,
> The fam'ly of God.

From the door of an orph'nage to the house of the King,
No longer an outcast; a new song I sing.
From rags unto riches, from the weak to the strong,
I'm not worthy to be here, but praise God, I belong!

> I'm so glad I'm a part of the fam'ly of God!
> I've been washed in the fountain,
> Cleansed by His blood.
> Joint heirs with Jesus as we travel this sod,
> For I'm part of the fam'ly,
> The fam'ly of God.

The Family of God

It was Good Friday and the kids had come home early from school. We had just put the Easter eggs we had dyed on Thursday night in the big yellow basket filled with shredded paper grass when the phone rang. A voice on the other end of the line said, "There's been an explosion at the Faust garage. Ronnie Garner was badly burned. He got out of the building just before it blew apart. But he isn't expected to make it through the night. Some of us are gathering at the church to pray. Call someone else, ask them to pray and to keep the prayer chain going."

I hung up the phone and called Bill at the office. I gathered the children around to pray for this young father from our church. Then I called a few others I knew would join us in prayer.

Only later did we get the rest of the story. Ron was working overtime because he and Darlene needed extra money to pay for heart surgery for their daughter Rachael. He was alone at the car dealership and repair shop, cleaning engines with a highly flammable substance without thinking to open a window for ventilation. He was working below a ceiling furnace with an open-flame pilot light. When the fumes from the solvent reached the flame, the whole garage blew apart. When he heard the first roar of the furnace, Ron tried to open the garage door, but it was jammed. By some miracle, with his clothing on fire, he managed to squeeze through a tiny space before the big explosion.

From Methodist Burn Center in Indianapolis we heard that the doctors had decided not to treat Ron; it was no use. There was little chance of success, and the trauma of treatment itself could push him over the edge. But friends who gathered at the church prayed all the more fervently for Ron, for Darlene, and for their two little girls. All through Friday and Saturday night, the church prayed. With part of our hearts we believed, but, to be honest, with the other part we braced ourselves for the predicted news.

A weary and somewhat tattered group gathered for church on Sunday morning. We lacked the optimism typical of an Easter celebration. The pastor wasn't there at first; we knew he was with Darlene and the family. No one felt like singing songs of victory. Resurrection seemed a million light-years away. But as the music began, a few weak voices sang less than harmonious chords of well-worn Easter songs.

As we were making an effort at worship, our pastor entered from the back and made his way up the center aisle to the platform. His shoulders looked tired, his suit was wrinkled, but there was a glow on his stubbled face as he motioned for us to stop the hymn. "Ron is alive," he said. "They said he wouldn't make it through Friday night, so they're amazed he's alive today. The doctors don't understand how he's hanging on, but we do, don't we? And because he's still alive, they've decided to start treatment."

A chorus of "Amen!" and "Praise the Lord" rose from the congregation. We all straightened in our seats like wilted plants that had been watered.

"We're going to thank the Lord," Pastor McCurdy said, "and then we're going to see this thing through. This is just the beginning. There will be many needs. The family will need food brought in. Darlene may need help with the kids. They may need transportation back and forth to Indianapolis. Ron will need gallons of blood for transfusions. And they all — the doctors, too — need prayer. Let's think of how each of us can help. We are, after all, the family of God. Now let's pray."

We stood and as one voice thanked God for answered prayer and for the reality of the Resurrection. Sunshine streamed in through the windows to warm more than our faces and the room. It seemed that the light of the dawn of the very first Easter morning had come to our weary souls.

What a service of rejoicing we had! No sermon could have spoken as articulately as the news of Ron's life and answered prayer. We sang the old hymn: "Low in the grave He lay, Jesus, my Savior. . . . He tore the bars away, Jesus, my Lord! Up from the grave He arose . . . With a mighty triumph o'er his foes!" My, how we sang!

And then, "You ask me how I know He lives? He lives within my heart!"

We were full of joy and victory as we left the church that noon, loading up our families into cars for the trip home.

In the car Bill and I said to each other, "You know, the amazing thing is, they'd do that for us, too." We weren't model church members, Bill and I. We were gone virtually every weekend, barely getting in from a concert in time to make it to church Sunday morning. We were never there to bake pies for the bake sales or to attend the couples' retreats or to teach in Bible school. If you had to pull your share of the load to get the family of God to take care of you, we would surely have been left out. "But they'd do that for us," we marveled.

When we got home, I checked the roast in the oven, changed the babies, and sent Suzanne off to put on her play clothes. Bill went to the piano, and I heard him toying with a simple, lovely tune. "Honey, come here a minute," he called from the family room.

He sang a phrase, "I'm so glad I'm a part of the family of God. Dah, dah, dah, la la la-la, la la la-la."

I grabbed a yellow legal pad and a pencil. The roast was forgotten as we were both consumed by the beauty of "the family," and I put our hearts into words:

> *Now you'll notice we say "brother" and "sister" round here;*
> *It's because we're a family and these folks are so near.*
> *When one has a heartache we all share the tears,*
> *And rejoice in each victory in the family so dear.*
> *I'm so glad I'm a part of the family of God. . .*

We finally did have Sunday dinner, though the roast was a little overdone. On Monday I deviled our Easter eggs, and our life went on, but we were never quite the same.

Pastor McCurdy was right; that Sunday news was only the beginning. But, then, the Resurrection was only a beginning, too! There were months of trips to Indianapolis. Many made casseroles and baby-sat and cleaned Darlene's house. Most sent cards of encouragement and notes assuring the Garners of continued prayer.

Ron had many skin grafts and experienced much pain, but finally he came home to their house on John Street. Eventually, he went back to Anderson College and finished his degree in athletics. He became assistant coach at Alexandria High School and fathered two more children. Rachael got her heart fixed and is now a high school teacher. And one of the children, not yet born at the time of the fire, is one of the top female athletes in the state of Indiana.

And I am filled with joy that the same Family that stood by the Garners in a thousand ways has stood by us, too. We don't deserve it; we haven't earned it. We were just born into it. They treat us like royalty, because we are! We're children of the King!

From the door of an orphanage to the house of the King;
No longer an outcast; a new song I sing.
From rags unto riches, from the weak to the strong,
I'm not worthy to be here, but praise God, I belong.

The King Is Coming

The marketplace is empty—no more traffic in the streets;
All the builders' tools are silent—no more time to harvest wheat.
Busy housewives cease their labors; in the courtroom no debate;
Work on earth is all suspended, as the King comes through the gate.

The railroad cars are empty as they rattle down the tracks,
In the newsroom no one watches as machines type pointless facts;
All the planes veer off their courses; no one sits at the controls,
For the King of all the ages comes to claim eternal souls.

Happy faces line the hallways; those whose lives have been redeemed,
Broken homes that He has mended, those from prison He has freed.
Little children and the aged hand in hand stand all aglow,
Who were crippled, broken, ruined, clad in garments white as snow.

> *The King is coming! The King is coming!*
> *I just heard the trumpet sounding and now His face I see,*
> *Oh, the King is coming! The King is coming!*
> *Praise God, He's coming for me!*

I can hear the chariots' rumble; I can see the marching throng.
The flurry of God's trumpets spells the end of sin and wrong.
Regal robes are now unfolding; heaven's grandstand's all in place—
Heaven's choirs, now assembled, start to sing, "Amazing Grace"!

> *The King is coming! The King is coming!*
> *I just heard the trumpet sounding and now His face I see,*
> *Oh, the King is coming! The King is coming!*
> *Praise God, He's coming for me!*

The King Is Coming

In 1970 Bill and I weren't thinking a great deal about the second coming of Christ. Our third baby had just been born. We were traveling and singing on weekends and, like most young couples, thinking a lot more about beginnings than about endings. We very much believed that Jesus would return one day to take God's family home, but our writing seemed to concentrate more on what God could do in a life now and how serving Him could make a difference in the choices we make and the priorities we keep.

An evangelist friend, Chuck Millhuff, and song evangelist, Jim Bohi, stopped by our house one day for dinner. We were discussing various ideas, and Bill mentioned a sermon on the Second Coming preached by another great evangelist, Jim Crabtree. We had not heard the sermon, but had heard about the urgency of his message — that, though we often lose sight of this truth in the busyness of our modern lives, Jesus *is* coming back. Jim had heard this particular sermon and described how evangelist Crabtree had ended the service by walking through the congregation, much like a town crier of early colonial America, saying, "The King is coming! The King is coming!"

We talked together about how important it was for people — young and old — to live as if Jesus would return any day — to set our goals, make our choices, raise our children, conduct business with the perspective of the imminent return of our Lord.

How could we capture the excitement of that truth in a song that might be as urgent as this great evangelist's message?

We began discussing how ordinary the day of Jesus' return would be. Chuck suggested a few images, such as the unfolding of the most regal robes and the assembling of the greatest choir ever gathered.

When Chuck and Jim left that day, Bill and I continued to talk about the return of Christ — as it would relate to the world in which we lived and functioned. How would it be for the people we knew, the life we all lived on a daily basis?

Bill tends to express his soul best with music, and before long he was looking for a musical setting that would fit such an idea, something simple and yet grand — like a coronation procession. For him, the chorus of a song is usually the first music to come, the setting for the theme. In this case we knew we wanted to do in a song what had been done in the sermon — to run through the streets of our world, so to speak, and alert folks that the King is coming! So the chorus was written: "The King is coming! The King is coming!"

At that time our office was in our house, with people coming and going all day. But even with three babies to care for and the phone ringing, I couldn't get this idea out of my mind. Bill's music ran through my brain as I fixed lunches and washed dishes and answered phones.

Suddenly, the ideas started to form themselves into poetry that seemed to be dictated to me. I put Benjy in the bassinet, let Amy play at my feet, grabbed a pencil, and started to write as fast as I could:

The marketplace is empty.
No more traffic in the streets.
All the builders' tools are silent.
No more time to harvest wheat.
Busy housewives cease their labors.
In the courtroom, no debate.
Work on earth has been suspended.
As the King comes through the gate.

Previously I had tended to think of the end of the world as a time of judgment, but that day I thought of all the beautiful endings to people's life stories that Satan had tried — but failed — to ruin. I thought of Jesus as the Master of restoration — of marriages He had put back together, relationships His hand had mended, generation gaps His Spirit had bridged. I saw an image of the coronation of a King who walked down the corridor of history; lining that corridor I could see the throngs of witnesses to His redeeming grace.

Happy faces line the hallways —
Those whose lives have been redeemed,
Broken homes that He has mended,
Those from prison He has freed.

Little children and the aged
Hand in hand stand all aglow,
Who were crippled, broken, ruined,
Clad in garments white as snow.

I saw the image of a great procession. This Great Redeemer who came first as a helpless baby, choosing the confines of human form — this Living Truth who chose to articulate His message with the limited expression of human language — would come again. This time He would not whimper from a manger or groan from a cross. It would not be a "silent night." This time Jesus would come in blinding glory as the King of all kings and Lord of lords! Never in all of history had there been an entry like this!

As I wrote, Chuck's images came again to my mind, and I included them with the lines that poured onto the paper.

I can hear the chariots rumble,
I can see the marching throng.
The flurry of God's trumpets
Spells the end of sin and wrong.
Regal robes are now unfolding,
Heaven's grandstand's all in place,
Heaven's choirs, now assembled,
Start to sing "Amazing Grace"!

When the lyric was written, I felt spent, yet shaky with excitement. I took the words in to Bill, and he immediately played and sang them, fitting them like a glove to the music he'd been hearing. His chorus finished the piece with simplicity and power.

We would have experiences similar to this again — those rare times when we knew God had given something to us that we could not claim as our own. Whether anyone ever sang the song or not, we had heard something important from the Father and we, at least, had to adjust our lives to embrace a Truth bigger than ourselves or a song.

Over the years many artists have recorded "The King Is Coming," and we ourselves have sung it hundreds of times in concert. It always has an impact on the audience that can only be described as ordained.

One of these days, we or someone else will sing it for the last time. The sound of the trumpets on the stage will be drowned out by one great blast from Michael's trumpet; instead of trying to imagine the return of our Lord, we shall "see the Son of man coming in a cloud with power and great glory" (Luke 21:27 KJV).

"For the Lord himself shall descend from heaven with a shout, with the voice of the archangel, and with the trump of God: and the dead in Christ shall rise first: Then we which are alive and remain shall be caught up together with them in the clouds, to meet the Lord in the air: and so shall we ever be with the Lord" (1 Thess. 4:16–17 KJV).

Comfort one another with these words: The King is coming!

The Old Rugged Cross
Made the Difference

'Twas a life filled with aimless desperation;
Without hope walk'd the shell of a man.
Then a hand with a nailprint stretch'd downward;
Just one touch! Then a new life began.

> And the old rugged cross made the difference
> In a life bound for heartache and defeat;
> I will praise Him forever and ever,
> For the cross made the difference in me.

Barren walls echoed harshness and anger;
Little feet ran in terror to hide.
Now those walls ring with love, warmth, and laughter,
Since the Giver of Life moved inside.

There's a room filled with sad, ashen faces;
Without hope death has wrapp'd them in gloom.
But at the side of a saint there's rejoicing,
For life can't be sealed in a tomb.

> And the old rugged cross made the difference
> In a life bound for heartache and defeat;
> I will praise Him forever and ever,
> For the cross made the difference in me.

The Old Rugged Cross
Made the Difference

*F*anny Crosby once wrote:

This is my story, this is my song,
Praising my Savior all the day long.

We are all storytellers. The regular days of our lives gradually weave themselves into a drama; most writers are simply observers and tellers of the stories that are all around them.

When we are young, we are given a lot of advice and instruction. Parents, teachers, preachers, and friends fill us with information about life. But those lessons are illustrated or refuted by the *story* told as we watch people make choices and observe the unfolding consequences of those choices.

I think of the stories of four men. The first was a young father named Bob, who was an explosion waiting to happen. He was gifted with his hands and had a bright mind, but he felt as if his life were an endless cycle of meaningless activity. Eat, sleep, go to work, come home, and start again. He had a well-paying job, a wife who loved him, and three beautiful children, but his days were full of frustration which he vented at home to those he loved best. Weekend parties only served to increase his sense of dissatisfaction, for once the alcohol haze wore off, the emptiness still gnawed at his soul.

His wife and children tried to stay out of his way; they learned to not make waves when he was in a bad mood. During those rare moments when he was happy, they absorbed his affections like a sponge, but eventually they learned to be wary even then. His personality could change as quickly as the weather during tornado season on the plains.

Several people invited Bob to church, but he didn't want anything to do with it. He'd attended as a kid, and he'd long ago walked away from the restrictions of that! But at this loving church the people kept praying for Bob. His wife took the children to church in spite of Bob's opposition, and one day she convinced him to go with her to a concert of a singer named Doug Oldham. A concert wouldn't be too religious, Bob thought, so he went. Besides, he was feeling guilty about his ugly disposition at home and wanted to make it up to his wife.

The music was upbeat, and the crowd seemed to really be into it. Bob loved music and found himself clapping along. About halfway through the concert, the singer told his story — how he used to be so hard to live with and so selfish that his wife finally took their children and left him, how he had contemplated suicide when faced with the reality of what he had done to a family that had loved him.

Bob could hardly believe what he was hearing. It could have been his story. It was as if the singer knew what was going on inside him — the way he did things he down deep didn't really mean (though he seemed powerless to stop himself), the way he was hurting the family he loved, the way he felt empty and helpless to change his life.

Bob knew he had to change direction, and he knew he was powerless to do it, as if he were all bound up inside. As Doug had sung, he was

Shackled by a heavy burden,
'Neath a load of guilt and shame...

But the song continued:

Then the hand of Jesus touched me
And now I am no longer the same!

He touched me; Oh He touched me!
And oh, the joy that floods my soul....

Joy! That was it. His life had no joy.

Bob talked to the pastor after the concert about his soul, but he wasn't ready to surrender his life. He'd had too much pain in his childhood — some related to church — and he wanted to make sure that if he started something, it would be "the real thing."

Some months later his wife convinced him to go with her to a revival that was sweeping a nearby college campus. Doug Oldham, the singer he'd heard at the concert, was to sing. Bob never got to hear the singer that night. The power of prayer was so strong at the beginning of the service that he knew he had to respond. He made his way to the altar. Doug saw him coming and met him there. Together they prayed that God would change Bob from the inside out. He did! And what a change!

Bob was a new man. He never took another drink. His anger began to subside. His lifelong habit of smoking stopped that night. His family could hardly believe the change in him at home. One day his little daughter said to her mother, "Something's happened to Daddy! He's not mad anymore." She was right. He was becoming a walking example of Paul's words, "If any man be in Christ, he is a new creature: old things are passed away; behold, all things are become new" (2 Cor. 5:17 KJV).

Not long after Bob told his story at our local church, Bill and I attended two funerals in our small town. The first was that of a man who had lived a selfish, reckless life. He had destroyed most of his relationships and had damaged people who got close to him. He died cursing those who tried to help him and refused all efforts at reconciliation. The visitors to the funeral home were few, and those who came were uncomfortable. What does one say? For those who had to live with him, there seemed more relief and guilt than genuine grief. There were no words of hope. The tone of the room was depressing, indeed.

The other funeral was after the death of Bill's grandfather, Grover Gaither, a simple man who lived what we thought was an ordinary life. A man of quiet integrity, his word was his contract. He had farmed a small Indiana farm and, when younger, worked in a factory. On weekends he traveled with Bill, Danny, and me, when the Gaither Trio sang in churches. He and Blanche never missed a service in their church; they supported their pastors; they housed evangelists and missionaries in their farmhouse. I'm sure Grover would have told you he had had a good life, though he had never done anything very spectacular.

How surprised we all were to see the funeral home packed with people of all ages. They filed by Grover's casket to tell stories. "He put me through electrical school," said one middle-aged man. "I stayed at their house when I had no place to go," said another. "He always cut my hair on Saturdays," said a young boy from the neighborhood. Each person went on to say something about Grover being "a good man" and how he had quietly impacted that person's life in practical ways.

There was much laughter and storytelling, too, reminiscent of Grover's great sense of humor. And great rejoicing! The tears of sadness were shed through smiles, remembering a man who had "died with his boots on" and his fields ready for planting, come spring.

Bob's story. Doug's story. The story of a sad, wasted life. Grover's story. My story. Your story. How it is told in the end and what the story says depends on what each of us does with Jesus.

For us, it has been the stories told — and lived — by real people that convinced us to stay with the way of the Cross. These stories made their way into a song we called "The Old Rugged Cross Made the Difference." For us, it truly has.

I Could Never Outlove the Lord

There've been times when giving and loving brought pain,
And I promised I would never let it happen again;
But I found out that loving was well worth the risk,
And that even in losing, you win.

I'm going to live the way He wants me to live;
I'm going to give until there's just no more to give;
I'm going to love, love 'til there's just no more love;
I could never, never outlove the Lord.

He showed us that only through dying we live,
And He gave when it seemed there was nothing to give;
He loved when loving brought heartache and loss;
He forgave from an old rugged cross.

I'm going to live the way He wants me to live;
I'm going to give until there's just no more to give;
I'm going to love, love 'til there's just no more love;
I could never, never outlove the Lord.

I Could Never
Outlove the Lord

I 've had it with him!" Bill said as he came through the back door. "He just takes and takes and takes. It would be different if I could ever see him maturing, but working with him is like pouring water in a sieve!" Bill disappeared into the bedroom, then came out in his Bermuda shorts. "I'm going out to mow."

There wasn't much for me to say. He was right. Our friend did seem to be so immature, and I'd watched Bill being "used" over and over. It seemed that this normally long-suffering man I had married was at the end of his patience. This time he'd been "done in"; it seemed to me our friend had gone beyond simple immaturity to what bordered on dishonesty.

Round and round the yard went the mowing tractor. Bill had a habit of doing his heavy problem-solving while mowing the grass or cutting branches or picking up pine cones in the yard.

But it wasn't long before I heard the motor stop. Bill walked into the kitchen, where I was feeding our little girl her lunch.

"You know what I'm going to do about that?" He rightly assumed I knew what "that" meant.

I waited.

"I'm going to keep on doing just what I've been doing. I'm going to keep on giving and loving and forgiving him. What else can I do? As long as God keeps giving grace and forgiveness to me, I don't have a choice."

What came next was a line that has been repeated very often in our home over the years. "After all, we could never outlove the Lord," Bill said.

Together we talked about how this truth could be lived out in this particular situation. And it wasn't long before we were in the family room by the piano putting the goodness of the Lord into a song. We recounted the times God had been a patient Friend, forgiving Father, gracious Counselor to us. In that session we also talked about the limits of our responsibility — our "job description" in matters of the soul. We reminded ourselves that loving, forgiving, "going the second mile" were our responsibility. Changing hearts, shaping minds, transforming "natures" were God's responsibility.

As I expect most people would, we asked ourselves where the limits were. Are there limits? We felt directed to a similar situation, where Peter asked Jesus, "So, how many times do I forgive? As many as seven times?" In Scripture *seven* is often used as the perfect number. Did Peter choose this number thinking he was being greatly generous with his mercy? For him did this represent the far-out limit of human perfection?

Jesus' answer blew Peter away. "Not seven times must you forgive, but seventy times seven." He seemed to be calling for perfection to an infinite multiple; He seemed to be asking Peter to limit himself only by the limits of his source of grace and forgiveness.

Did Jesus also teach confrontation? Yes. Did He model teaching and giving direction? Yes. But always He modeled forbearance, patience, and a belief in the positive potential of what the worst human being could become. *Go, and sin no more. . . . Return home. . . . Your faith has made you whole. . . . Neither do I condemn you. . . . This day you shall be with me in paradise.* These are examples of how Jesus handled those who had been in the wrong.

That day we finished the song "I Could Never Outlove the Lord." We went on doing what we'd been doing. And God went on doing what He does. We are still friends with the person Bill pondered on the tractor. He is still in the process of becoming what God has in mind. He has been greatly used by the Lord to reach hundreds of people we could never have reached. Is he perfect? Not yet. Are we perfect? Far from it.

But what God has started in all of us He has promised to finish. And now, twenty-five years after that day at the crossroads of a friendship, we are finding it is still true: We could never, never outlove the Lord.

Maybe one day Bill and I will write one of those little books of practical insights and call it "Treasures from the Tractor!"

The Church Triumphant

This old ship's been thru battles
  before,
Storms and tempests and rocks on
  the shore,
Though the hull may be battered,
Inside it's safe and dry,
It will carry its cargo
To the port in the sky.

Let the Church be the Church!
Let the people rejoice!
For we've settled the question;
We've made our choice.
Let the anthem ring out!
Songs of victory swell!
For the Church triumphant
Is alive and well.

God has always had a people. Many a foolish conqueror has made the mistake of thinking that because he had driven the church of Jesus Christ out of sight, he had stilled its voice and snuffed out its life. But God has always had a people. The powerful current of a rushing river is not diminished because it is forced to flow underground; the purest water is the stream that bursts crystal clear into the sunlight after it has forced its way through solid rock!

There have been charlatans who, like Simon the magician, sought to barter on the open market that power which cannot be bought or sold, but God has always had a people, men who could not be bought and women who were beyond purchase. God has always had a people!

There have been times of affluence and prosperity when the Church's message has been nearly diluted into oblivion by those who sought to make it socially attractive, neatly organized, and financially profitable. It has been gold-plated, draped in purple, and encrusted with jewels. It has been misrepresented, ridiculed, lauded, and scorned. These followers of Jesus Christ have been, according to the whim of the times, elevated as sacred leaders or martyred as heretics, yet through it all there marches on that powerful army of the meek, God's chosen people, who cannot be bought, flattered, murdered, or stilled! On through the ages they march. The Church, God's Church triumphant, is alive and well!

The Church Triumphant

My parents pastored struggling churches in small Michigan towns all their ministering years. Their gift and calling seemed to be establishing new congregations and building a firm foundation by teaching and nurturing believers. Some places were very difficult. Others were a joy. All took long-term commitment. Isolation was a reality of their lives. These churches were in out-of-the-way places, and there was often little fellowship or encouragement for pastors like them.

But every June our family made an annual pilgrimage to our church's international convention — or "camp meeting," as it was called. It was often the oasis of fellowship in a desert of the soul. And the trip always gave my parents assurance that the body of Christ was a grand living organism with many body parts, functioning in harmony with

Christ, the Head. This "bigger picture" kept them going when it seemed all they could see were "kneecaps" and "elbows."

Bill, too, grew up in a small church, in a farm community in Indiana. Here, as a young boy, he first played piano and, as a college student, directed the volunteer choir. Here he gained experience as a worship leader and an organizer of singing groups — trios, quartets, ensembles.

He saw pastors who sometimes lost heart and perspective until some traveling evangelist or missionary came to town to give the believers there a view of God at work in the larger world. The outsiders would tell stories or show slides that brought encouragement and inspired the folks to see the "field white unto harvest" beyond the city limits of their small Midwestern town.

Over the years Bill and I have been privileged to see a broad spectrum of God's beautiful family. And because we both know what it feels like to be isolated and discouraged, one of our passions and joys has been helping God's big family come to know how much we need one another.

Every time a new person comes to God, every time someone's gifts find expression in the fellowship of believers, every time a family in need is surrounded by the caring church, the truth is affirmed anew: the Church triumphant is alive and well!

Someone has said that the Church at its very worst is better than the world at its best. We have found that to be true. We are not perfect people, but we are people in whom God has begun a good work, and He has promised He will "keep right on helping [us] grow in his grace until his task within [us] is finally finished on that day when Jesus Christ returns" (Phil. 1:6 LB).

Through the centuries there have been those who overtly tried to destroy the church of Jesus. Enemies of the Cross have tried to discredit its story. Tyrants have tried to wipe it out by killing those who believed, mistakenly thinking that they could kill Truth by destroying those who told the truth. Others have diluted its message until the truth was barely recognizable, not comprehending that the church of Jesus Christ is not a situational ethic but a living organism.

But in all the climates of history, there have been those true believers who have quietly settled in their hearts to set their sights on a better kingdom. They have staked their lives on the promise that if their earthly bodies, "this tabernacle," were dissolved, they would still have "a building of God, a house not made with hands, eternal in the heavens" (2 Cor. 5:1 KJV).

Bill and I wrote this song to encourage believers like those I knew in my parents' churches and Bill knew as a young Christian boy — believers who serve God in out-of-the-way places in obscure settings. And as we ourselves have sometimes felt isolated and alone or sometimes overwhelmed by the immensity of the needs and the limits of our abilities to affect them, we, too, have been reminded, by singing this song, of the bigger picture: God is at work and we are only called to be faithful where we are. The Church is His body, and it is alive and well!

Jesus Is Lord of All

All my tomorrows, all my past —
Jesus is Lord of all;
I've quit my struggle, contentment at last —
Jesus is Lord of all.

All of my conflicts, all my thoughts —
Jesus is Lord of all;
His love wins the battles I could not have fought.
Jesus is Lord of all.

All of my longings, all my dreams —
Jesus is Lord of all.
All my failures His power redeems.
Jesus is Lord of all.

King of kings, Lord of lords,
Jesus is Lord of all.
All my possessions and all my life —
Jesus is Lord of all.

Jesus Is Lord of All

*I*t was June and the week of Amy's third birthday. To celebrate she wanted to have a cookout down at the creek. She planned her own menu: hot dogs and hamburgers, corn on the cob, green beans, watermelon, and raspberry cake.

The afternoon of the big affair, Grandma and Grandpa were the first to arrive. Benjy, then almost two, had a brand-new ball and bat and wanted Grandma to play ball with him. So while Amy waited for the cousins to climb into the wagon we had hitched to the garden tractor, Benjy and Grandma went on down to play ball.

The older children rode on the tractor and in the wagon with Bill, going by the road, and I walked down the hillside with a pot of hot coffee. I could see Grandma and Benjy under the willow tree, Grandma pitching and Benjy up at bat. This lovely scene warmed my heart.But suddenly the mood was shattered when I saw Benjy throw his bat on the ground, stomp his angry little feet, and yell at the top of his lungs, "Grandma! You missed again! You missed my bat again!"

It turned out to be that kind of day for this little guy. Nothing went the way he wanted. He wanted it to be his birthday, but it was Amy's. He wanted to eat watermelon when we were roasting hot dogs. He wanted to go for a paddle-boat ride, but everyone else was running races. By the end of the day, with all the playing, running, fighting, and crying, Benjy was exhausted.

He held his arms up to me and said, "Carry me, Mommy," so I carried him up the hillside to the house. He was all hot and dirty, and he went to sleep on my shoulder before I got him to the top.

I took him to his room and laid him on his green bedspread. How dear he looked — his blond hair all plastered to his forehead, catsup on his nose, a grubby little baseball clutched tightly in one hand! How I loved him! I took the baseball from his clenched fingers and smiled to myself as I remembered what he had said earlier about missing his bat.

Then, as I stood there beside that exhausted little boy, now holding his toy in my hand, I became aware of some struggles of my own, some areas in my life that I needed to relinquish.

There had been times when I had acted like a spiritual two-year-old. Times when I had stood with my own neat little set of needs and longings and desires in my hand and, in my own more subtle and sophisticated way, shouted at my children and my husband and the church and others around me, "You missed my bat! Here I am, with my needs all ready to be met, and you missed my bat."

I recognized the weariness I felt in my soul. I'd been there before. This was a weariness that comes from struggle over lordship in an area of my life. Perhaps I had let it go on so long this time because it involved my children and Bill. I knew well that "whoever tries to keep his life will lose it," but it was not so easy to apply that principle to those dearest to me in all the world. Houses and lands and cars and plans — I could hold those loosely. My family? Not so easy. In my *head* I knew that, in holding them tightly, I might lose them forever. But in practice, I held them in little ways: making them need me, burdening them with the awareness that I needed them — subtle little ways of keeping them for myself and my needs and my fulfillment.

So that day beside a sleeping little boy, I knelt and gave it all up to Jesus: our precious children, our marriage, our hopes and plans and dreams and schemes, my fears and failures — all of it. Once more the peace and contentment came as I began to cease the struggling.

I wish I could say that was the last time I had to learn that Jesus must be Lord. The truth is that as soon as we relinquish one area of our lives, God seems to make us aware of new unsurrendered areas. This process caused us to write a song that we have sung at many other such junctures in our lives. We wrote "Jesus Is Lord of All" to encourage us, too, when Satan would try to use a past failure as an accusation.

I remember a friend once comparing this growth process to the gift of an antique book. "Suppose I found and bought for you a beautiful rare book," he said, "and put it away until I saw you. When I gave it to you, you were delighted with this treasure, and I felt pleased to have given it to you. But some time later, I was cleaning out the drawer where I had kept the book and found some fragile pages that had fallen out. I called you and said, 'I'm so sorry, but I overlooked some pages of that gift I gave you. I will bring them to you. I want you to have everything.'"

Let's say the antique book represents our lives that we give — surrender — to the lordship of Christ. But it seems that sometimes the great accuser takes such an occasion as opportunity to say, "Well, you're a failure. See, you didn't really give the gift — the book — to your friend. You didn't really want Him to have it at all." If we're talking about an antique book, we could see how ridiculous such an accusation would be. But when it comes to giving Jesus lordship of our lives, we are often confused by the same ugly accusation.

God wants to teach us that when we commit our lives to Him, He gives us that wonderful teacher, the Holy Spirit. He will lead us in the constant pursuit of giving every area of our lives to the control of Him who treasures the rare gift that we are, for God made each of us a unique creation and wants to be the lover of our souls.

Whenever we thwart the work He has begun in us, we rob ourselves of all God intended for us to have and be. If we will let him, though, He has promised to share with us all He is. Second Peter 1:3–4 (NEB) says it this way:

> His divine power has bestowed on us everything that makes for life and true religion, enabling us to know the One who called us by His own splendor and might. Through this might and splendor He has given us His promises, great beyond all price, and through them you may escape the corruption with which

lust has infected the world, and come to share in the very being of God.

When the God of the universe offers to share with each of us all He is, that's a good deal!

It's Beginning to Rain

(from Joel 2:28–32 and Acts 2:17–21)

The turtle dove is singing its sweet song of mourning;
The leaves on the trees turn their silver cups to the sky.
The silent clouds above are beginning to gather;
The barren land is thirsty,
And so am I.

The young man's eyes start to shine as he tells of his vision;
The old understand what he sees for they've dreamed their dreams.
With the thrill of being alive, they reach for each other,
And they dance in the rain with the joy
Of the things that they've seen.

At the first drop of rain that you hear, throw open the windows;
Go call all your children together and throw wide the door!
When the rains of the Spirit are falling, fill every vessel,
For he who drinks his fill will thirst no more.

It's beginning to rain —
Hear the voice of the Father,
Saying, "Whosoever will
Come drink of this water;
I have promised to pour My Spirit out
On your sons and your daughters.
If you're thirsty and dry,
Look up to the sky —
It's beginning to rain."

It's Beginning to Rain*

I've always loved water. Nothing quiets my spirit and makes me feel like I'm where I belong so much as a body of water. I love the flowing river that meanders through meadows and fields, forests and cities; I love its quiet power, cutting through granite, gouging out canyons, slicing through mountains, moving whole civilizations. I love the questions the river raises. Where have I been? Where am I going? What will I carry with me? I love its certainty and resoluteness. You don't change the river, said Mark Twain. The river goes where the river goes on its way to the sea.

I love lakes, still and mysterious, calming and secretive, mirroring everything along their shores, calling the children to skip rocks and the fishermen to skip work. I love the spring-fed cold of lakes, the amniotic, life-sustaining smell of them. I love the sound of birds breaking the water's surface in search of minnows and fish flopping up to catch water

---

* The theme (Joel 2:28–29) for this song was brought to us by friend and co-writer Aaron Wilborn.

bugs and insects. I love the sound of water lapping at the bottom of a fishing boat after dark and of paddles dipping deep and strong to bring weary children back to the lakeshore.

But most of all I love the sea. I love the beauty and the terror of it. I love the certainty and the uncertainty of it, its amazing power and its sweet gentleness. It reminds me never to limit myself to believing merely in the possible, and most of all, never to limit God to what seems "possible." It reminds me that a God who can be explained by my mind is no God at all, but an idol constructed by my own hands or, worse, a house pet led on a leash. I must stand beside the ocean often so I will not forget that I am not the creator of the universe and that I must never create God in my image. His ways are immensely higher than my ways.

When I worry about relationships that seem to come and go, I must let the tide teach me that there is an ebb and flow to everything, and that the tide that goes out will, in due time, return if I just trust the God who sets the boundaries and is the measure of all things.

I've heard the story of a man standing by the ocean and exclaiming, "Just look at all that water." His wisecracking friend replied, "Yes, and just think . . . that's just the top of it!"

Exactly! If the surface is an awesome thing, just consider the amazing, expansive depths. Scientists say we know more about outer space and the galaxies than we know about the wonders of the deep sea. One thing we know: Water is life. Without the sea there would be no life. From those bodies of water moisture is drawn into rain clouds that drop water onto the thirsty land. No plant life or animal life could survive without water. Water is everything to the survival of this earth.

I also love the rain. I love rainy days; that's when I feel most creative. I love fog and mist and downpours and sprinkles. I love storms with thunder and lightning and periwinkle purple skies. I love moisture frozen high in the atmosphere that sifts down on my face as snow.

I love water. I always thought we had it all wrong. If water is the most life-giving element on earth, then when rain comes we should all run out into it instead of running inside to get out of it. Instead of closing the windows and doors, we should fling them open to watch and hear and feel the life-sustaining gift being bestowed upon us all. We should gather our children and be bathed by the rain on our faces — and give thanks for the wonder of wonders.

Jesus said, "I am the Water of Life." All too often when the rains of His Spirit begin to fall, we reach for our umbrellas. When the lightning flashes around our churches and the voice of God thunders, we close the doors and stained-glass windows and worship the Good Shepherd who is safely depicted behind the baptistery.

But the Water of Life says, "In the last days I will pour out my spirit upon all flesh, and your sons and your daughters shall prophesy (preach!) and your old men will dream dreams, and your young men will see visions." When we begin to hear the thunder of old men becoming insightful, of young men becoming visionary, of young men or women delivering inspired messages, we should throw open the windows and fling wide the doors. We should gather our children and run into the streets, praying that the rains of the Water of Life will drench us all. We should splash and play in the puddles of fresh insights, swim in the lakes of renewal, and dive into the rivers of mercy. We should push out into the sea of God's amazing life-giving love. Can you feel the winds start to blow? Can you see the change in the sky and the trees? It's beginning to rain. The Water of Life is coming!

Gentle Shepherd

Gentle Shepherd, come and lead us,
For we need You to help us find our way.
Gentle Shepherd, come and feed us,
For we need Your strength from day to day.
There's no other we can turn to
Who can help us face another day;
Gentle Shepherd, come and lead us,
For we need You to help us find our way.

In a day when our ears are bombarded by beckoning voices and our world is polluted with sound, Lord, let us hear You.

In a land dissected and muddled by mazes of roads and never-ending highways, Lord, help us find Your way.

In a world of easy promises, empty guarantees, and quick-claim insurance policies, give us the security of Your hand, Lord Jesus.

At a time when we are confused by conflicting authorities that would tell us how to manage our marriages, our finances, and our children, Oh, Lord Jesus, show us Your way.

As we walk the tightropes of parenthood in these explosive days, training our little ones to live in a world for which there are no precedents, Lord, we just need You.

In all things, Gentle Shepherd, help us find the way.

There's no other we can turn to
Who can help us face another day;
Gentle Shepherd, come and lead us,
For we need You to help us find our way.

Gentle Shepherd

As I write this I am in a small cottage in England with my daughter Amy and her husband, Andrew, and their little son, Lee. Amy and Andrew, who recently finished their graduate degrees in theater and acting, had planned for a long time to visit the country that gave us William Shakespeare and many other great poets, novelists, and dramatists.

Their plan was to take a cottage for two weeks in the Cotswold hills, the rolling countryside in the heart of England that has remained relatively unchanged for centuries: the England you picture in your mind but assume must have disappeared long ago. From this central location they would take short trips, allowing them to absorb the settings and roots of much of the literature they have studied and performed. So I came along to enjoy England and help with — and enjoy — little Lee.

This is farmland and sheep country. The green fields are dotted with sheep and newborn lambs. Along the narrow roadways, a common sign reads: "Keep gates closed at all times." The shepherds explain that if one sheep gets out, the rest will follow, and once they're out, they become confused and easily scattered. They seem to not have "homing instincts" like dogs or geese. They get entangled in briers or fall into ditches. They eat things that make them sick and are vulnerable to attack by predators. And, perhaps worst of all, they are clueless that they are so clueless.

David the psalmist was a shepherd, so the songs he wrote are full of sheep metaphors and imagery. "The LORD is my shepherd, I shall not want" (Ps. 23:1 KJV), begins the most memorized chapter in all of Scripture, the psalm that goes on to compare every aspect of our lives to that of a sheep cared for by a wise and alert shepherd. Psalm 28 ends with David's plea, "Save your people and bless your inheritance; be their shepherd and carry them forever." In Psalm 119 the psalmist confesses, "I have strayed like a lost sheep" (v. 176).

Jesus, too, chose to call Himself a "shepherd" and referred to human beings in general and His disciples in particular as "sheep." When He saw the crowds of people so lost, so needy, He was moved with compassion for them "because they were harassed and helpless, like sheep without a shepherd" (Matt. 9:36). He told His disciples that a "good shepherd lays down his life for the sheep" (John 10:11), and that His passion for them was that they would be one flock with one shepherd.

All of these references to sheep have come flooding back into my mind this week as I have watched the contentment of sheep well fed and well protected on these lush Cotswold pastures where fresh, clear streams flow and where Cotswold-stone fences and thick, tall hedges keep the sheep from wandering and predators from intruding.

And yet as we drove along one narrow, too-well-traveled road, we were startled to go around a curve and see two sheep noses nibbling grass only inches from the roadway. They seemed oblivious to the danger. As long as there was a blade of grass to fill their stomachs, they naively nibbled their way toward destruction. How they needed a shepherd!

How like them we human beings are! When things seem fine from our limited point of view, we may actually be most threatened; because we are so complacent we don't feel a need for a shepherd.

But when we are panicked by life's problems, we may well be safer simply because we are then more aware of our need for a guide, a protector, a staff to keep us on the path to a destination we long for but could never find on our own.

We wrote this song "Gentle Shepherd" when we were beginning our parenting process. And in Bill's and my experience, nothing has made us more aware of our need for a shepherd than parenting the children God has given us. We, like the sheep, are sometimes so clueless. We don't know the sorts of personalities God is developing in our children. We can see only glimpses of their gifts and often recognize only those with which we can identify. The potential beyond that is hard to calculate. We are preparing them to live in a world we can only imagine; the vocations they will choose may not yet exist.

The balance of affirmation and discipline, freedom and restraint, encouragement and warning is different for each child and season and generation, yet the absolutes of God's Word are necessary and trustworthy no matter how mercuric the time. But how those principles can best be taught to various children at various ages and in various points in history is something that demands wisdom greater than any parent can have unless he or she is led by the Great Shepherd.

When I was a junior in high school, my mother wrote these words to me, encouraging me to turn to the Shepherd she followed:

The Shepherd Friend

The sheep may know the pasture,
But the Shepherd knows the sheep;
The sheep lie down in comfort,
But the Shepherd does not sleep.

He protects the young and foolish,
From their unprecocious way,
And gently prods the aged,
Lest they give in to the clay.

When the young have learned some wisdom,
It is much too late to act;
When the old man knows the method,
He is less sure of the fact.

Ah, the Shepherd knows the answer —
The beginning and the end.
So the wisest choice, my daughter,
Is to take Him as your friend.

—Dorothy Sickal

And long before our parents prayed for wisdom to lead and train us, before I felt as helpless as a sheep parenting my children, the prophet Isaiah wrote in detail about a Messiah who would be a gentle shepherd to every generation: "Say to the towns of Judah, 'Here is your God!' See, the Sovereign LORD comes with power, and his arm rules for him. . . . He tends his flock like a shepherd: He gathers the lambs in his arms and carries them close to his heart; he gently leads those that have young" (Isa. 40:9–11).

Now Bill and I are watching our children parent our three grandchildren. In one generation, things have changed drastically. Our children were among the first to see a "Speak n Spell," one of the early computer toys. Now our grandchildren (ages three and five) create stories, learn number concepts, and read their favorite books interactively on a powerful home computer on line to the Internet; they are very comfortable with the computer world. The world of these, our children's children, will be wildly different from the one we now know. Yet the Shepherd of our hearts will guide them, too, into green pastures of the soul and beside still waters of the Spirit.

A sheep never outgrows its need for a shepherd; a good shepherd never expects the sheep to be a shepherd, but knows that the sheep are simply sheep who need to be cared for until they die.

There's no other we can turn to
Who can help us face another day;
Gentle Shepherd, come and lead us,
For we need You to help us find our way.

It Is Finished

There's a line that's been drawn through the ages;
On that line stands the old rugged cross.
On that cross a battle is raging
For the gain of man's soul or its loss.

On one side march the forces of evil,
All the demons and devils of hell;
On the other the angels of glory,
And they meet on Golgotha's hill.

The earth shakes with the force of the conflict;
The sun refuses to shine,
For there hangs God's Son in the balance,
And then through the darkness He cries —

Yet in my heart the battle was raging;
Not all pris'ners of war have come home.
These were battlefields of my own making;
I didn't know that the war had been won.

Then I heard that the King of the Ages
Had fought all my battles for me,
And vict'ry was mine for the claiming,
And now, praise His name, I am free!

It is finished! The battle is over.
It is finished; there'll be no more war.
It is finished, the end of the conflict.
It is finished, and Jesus is Lord!

It Is Finished

Bill and I love to hear great orators as much as we love great literature. It has been our privilege to hear — in person or through the media — many great speakers. We'll never forget the milestone moment in our nation's history when Martin Luther King Jr. delivered the now famous "I Have a Dream" speech. Or the day John F. Kennedy spoke the words that began a fatal crack in the Berlin Wall: "Ich bin ein Berliner."

To teach English students the principle of communication, we used the eulogy delivered by Sen. Mike Mansfield, of Montana, after Kennedy was assassinated, "And she took a ring and placed it on his finger. . . ."

And who could forget ten thousand voices at the Praise Gathering for Believers in Indianapolis affirming in one great voice the truth Tony Campolo had drilled into our very souls: "It's Friday . . . Sunday's coming!"

Because we had learned to recognize and appreciate such moments, Bill and I knew that it was a timeless honor to sing at the same service in which nationally known radio orator B. R. Lakin was to deliver a sermon on Jesus' last words from the cross: "It is finished!"

It was hard to forget the way Dr. Lakin ended his message. "And the drops of blood from His precious hands seeped into the sand below the old rugged cross and said to the sand, 'It is finished.' The grains of sand whispered their message to the blades of grass, 'It is finished!' A little bird swooped down and plucked a blade of grass and flew to the top of the pine tree and carried the message to the uppermost branch, 'It is finished!' The pine standing like a sentinel raised its branches to the sky and repeated to the forests around and the clouds above, 'It is finished!' The heavens echoed the wondrous liberating news, 'It is finished!' until the winds blew across the sea and the waves lapping on the shore repeated the message to the farthest oceans, 'It is finished!'"

Bill and I were overwhelmed with the beauty and grandeur of this picture. Afterward, I wasn't surprised that Bill said, "We've got to write a song about that, Honey. 'It is finished!' What a great title!"

Even then my mind was exploding, stretching, asking, searching. *What was finished?* I couldn't escape the question. How could I ever hope to comprehend the scope of redemption and capture it in a song?

For a year I struggled. Bill kept saying, "Honey, we need to write that song."

I said, "Yes, we must. But I'm not ready. I can't distill this truth into four verses and a chorus. Let me live with it a while longer."

I read and reread the crucifixion story. Insight by insight I made the truths my own. The drink from the Messiah's cup on the Passover night in the Upper Room; the prayer Jesus prayed for His friends there and for us here. The betrayal by Judas, the denial by Peter. The inquisition, trial, and execution. The amazing last words of Jesus. I considered the implications of the troubling of the forces of nature: the earthquakes, the unnatural darkness, the strange storm. And I worked to comprehend how these chaotic eruptions in the natural realm were used to issue new proclamations in the spiritual realm: a torn barrier to the Holy of Holies, an opening of access to the mercy seat and the awesome presence of God, a redefining of the terms *royalty, priesthood, sacrifice, intermediary.*

At that time our nation was involved in the long and seemingly pointless Vietnam War. When "the conflict" was finally ended, a generation of America's young had been riddled. This was the only war I had known well. I was born after the bombing of Pearl Harbor, and I barely remembered the Korean War. Vietnam was my generation's war — the first war to pull the nation apart rather than unite it. It left both those who served in it and those who refused to serve confused and bewildered and at odds with one another. It was an ambiguous war.

I well remember the night Bill and I sat and wept in our living room as we watched on television the return home of prisoners of war from Vietnam. Some fell to the ground and kissed American soil. Others threw themselves into the arms of waiting parents, wives, and sweethearts who had lived in the fear that these soldiers would never come back. Some hugged their two-, three-, and four-year-old children whom they had never seen. The relief on the faces — the tears, the joy, the hope, the pain — was almost too much to bear.

About that same time Bill and I picked up a major news magazine that carried the story of another American soldier. This man had wandered out of the forest on some secluded island in the South Pacific. He was carrying a rusty weapon and was dressed in what remained of a tattered American uniform. He was suspicious and frightened, as authorities took him into custody. The article explained that this was a World War II soldier who had been lost from his company and left behind. No one had ever told him that the Allies had won the war, that he was free to go home, that victory had been declared long ago. All those years he had remained at war in his mind, fighting a battle that had already been won.

The song Bill wanted us to write was falling into place for me.

War — the cross of Jesus was about war, a war of cosmic proportions, the war of the ages. This was a war with a clear objective: freedom for every soul since Eden. It was a war fought on earth where mankind could see it, and a war fought in the unseen world, from the heavens to the very pit of hell. What was finished? I'd asked the question for a year. Bill had the music; now the words would come.

I saw the crack in the earth — caused by the quake that shook Golgotha — as a cosmic split in the universe, a line that divided all history and all time into B.C. and A.D. I began to write:

> *There's a line that's been drawn through the ages;*
> *On that line stands an old rugged cross.*
> *On that cross a battle is raging*
> *For the gain of man's soul or its loss.*

The sides and powers of the conflict were clearly defined. If there ever was a holy war, a righteous cause, this was it. And each of us had major stakes in this war's outcome.

On one side march the forces of evil,
All the demons and devils of hell;
On the other the angels of glory,
And they meet on Golgotha's hill.

The disturbances of nature — much more than a simple storm or earthquake. This earthquake shook the very foundations of the firmament and reverberated into eternity.

The earth shakes with the force of the conflict;
The sun refuses to shine,
For there hangs God's Son in the balance,
And then through the darkness He cries —

IT IS FINISHED! The battle is over.
IT IS FINISHED! There'll be no more war.
IT IS FINISHED! The end of the conflict.
IT IS FINISHED! And Jesus is Lord.

A defeated enemy is impotent. Every battle-weary soldier must be told: The war is over!

I thought of that poor, bedraggled man peering suspiciously out from the dark forest, afraid to come out into the sunlight, guarding his little island. I saw myself, and I suddenly realized that this is a picture of us all. Because of Jesus, Satan has no power over us unless he can keep us from hearing the news of the victory, unless he can convince us that the war has never been won.

Of all the declarations of freedom — the Magna Carta, the Declaration of Independence, the Bill of Rights — none has been written so eloquently or at such great cost in bloodshed as the one spoken in three words from an old rugged cross: IT IS FINISHED! Every isolated soldier of life's battle must hear it.

> *Yet in my heart the battle was raging;*
> *Not all prisoners of war have come home.*
> *These were battlefields of my own making,*
> *I didn't know that the war had been won.*
> *Then I heard that the King of the Ages*
> *Had fought all my battles for me.*
> *And the victory was mine for the claiming,*
> *And now, praise His name, I am free!*
> *IT IS FINISHED!*

Bill sat down at the piano, played his tune, and sang through the words on the yellow tablet in front of him. Tears ran down our faces as we embraced anew the truth that had set us free. We were coming to know at a sweeter, deeper level what was meant by the words the blade of grass whispered to the bird that day on Golgotha: *It is finished!*

We Have This Moment, Today

Hold tight to the sound of the music of living —
Happy songs from the laughter of children at play;
Hold my hand as we run through the sweet, fragrant meadows,
Making mem'ries of what was today.

For we have this moment to hold in our hands,
And to touch as it slips through our fingers like sand;
Yesterday's gone, and tomorrow may never come,
But we have this moment, today!

Tiny voice that I hear is my little girl calling
For Daddy to hear just what she has to say;
And my little son running there down the hillside,
May never be quite like today.

Tender words, gentle touch, and a good cup of coffee,
And someone that loves me and wants me to stay;
Hold them near while they're here, and don't wait for tomorrow
To look back and wish for today.

Take the blue of the sky and the green of the forest,
The gold and the brown of the freshly mown hay,
Add the pale shades of spring and the circus of autumn,
And weave you a lovely today.

For we have this moment to hold in our hands,
And to touch as it slips through our fingers like sand;
Yesterday's gone, and tomorrow may never come,
But we have this moment, today!

We Have This Moment, Today

W hat is your life?" asks James 4:14 (KJV). "It is even a vapor, that appeareth for a little time, and then vanisheth away."

Even children seem to know how short life is. "Don't go to work, Daddy," they beg. "Stay here with me today." But adults, knowing "what's important," go away for another business trip to make more contacts to sell more contracts to make more products that will be outdated before they can be shipped. And the child grows. And childhood vanishes . . . like a vapor.

"Suzanne will not be at school today," I once wrote to her teacher. "She stayed home to play with her mother." I don't remember many other days of her elementary years, but I remember that day.

When Bill and I first learned we were expecting our first grand-baby, little old ladies would stop us and say, "Oh, there's nothing like grandchildren; you haven't lived until you have grandchildren. You are so busy that you miss your children, but you enjoy your grandchildren."

We wanted to hit them! We had a life before grandchildren! We didn't *miss* our children; we savored the moments so much we could almost hear their bones grow. Grandkids would be nice, but they weren't that big of a deal.

Then Suzanne had her son, Will, and there into that cradle marched all the generations of Irish and German and English and Italian Sickals and Mahoneys and Kelleys and Hartwells and Allens and Gaithers and Jenningses and Smiths. There they were pouring into that tiny wiggling piece of delicate humanity with grandpa's nose and grandma's eyes and Mom's fingers and aunt's toes and uncle's kneecaps. Yet Will was none of them, but a very personal and unique mural all his own. Our child's child! All Suzanne's moments since we first held her in our arms were periscoped into this moment. We could hardly bear it. It was a knowing beyond comprehension, an expression beyond words. It was words made flesh, and that flesh had to be held; it could not be spoken.

Moments that matter are like that. They are as fragile as holding a snowflake on your warm tongue. Yet they are eternal somehow, like a purifying hot coal that brands your lips as if you were Isaiah, and you know you'll never be the same.

Three pieces of writing are now in my hand. One was written August 1, 1978. The second, June 23, 1993. The time between the two disappears like a vapor as I read them.

In the first, our daughter Amy is nine years old. We are sitting in the garden swing in our backyard. I have just peeled an apple and shared it with her, as we have done since she was a baby eating her first solid food. But today it is almost a sacrament. As we share the apple, I am telling her about the facts of life and reproduction in answer to her curious questions. She wants to know. She is afraid to know. I try to give her no more information than she can handle, yet be honest and truthful. Later that day I will write in my journal:

Amy and I had a long talk about the facts of life this week. I tried to lift the curtain of miracle for her and let her know that entering puberty is like crossing the threshold from the outer courtyard of innocence into the very holy of holies itself, experiencing with that step the pain and glory that comes with knowledge and responsibility. To realize that she carries in her body the potential to be co-creator with the God of the universe is an awesome and yet wonderful realization.

The laughter and tears that burst simultaneously from her little upturned face told me what an earthshaking moment this was for her. For me, this was one of the unique moments of my life that make me thrilled, thankful, and scared to death to be a mother.

Together we prayed that she would keep her vessel pure and clean. And we prayed for the child somewhere entering manhood who will someday be her husband — that God would protect and preserve him and bring him one day to her, so that together they could buck the tide of careless living to form a home that will be fortress and citadel, cathedral and synagogue, laughter and healing to some other child.

The second piece of writing is a letter. I wrote it the night before Amy's wedding to the young man who would be her husband.

Dear Andrew,

Years ago Amy and I sat in the garden swing and talked about the facts of life and the part her body would play in a marvelous mystery that was unfolding before and within her. Tears welled up in both our eyes as she began to understand the amazing plan God had for bringing together two people in the miracle of being co-creators with Him. It was almost more than she could fathom to discover that way back in the womb her body was being equipped and her development was directioned toward this realization.

That day after we talked, I held her in my arms in the swing and together we prayed for the little boy that was somewhere growing up who would one day be her husband. We asked God to protect him and save him for her and to give his parents the wisdom to help him become what God had in mind for him. We prayed that Amy would keep herself pure and unspoiled by the shoddy values of the world so that she would follow God's path all the way to this man when God's time had come.

We didn't know that day, and many times since, that we were praying for you, for your family, for your protection. How beautifully God has answered our prayers.

The third piece is not written by me. It is a note I received this week from Amy in Nebraska, where she and Andrew have just finished their graduate work. Soon they — and their young son, Lee — will move to a place of God's choosing.

Dear Mother,

I can't believe how much I love Lee and I can't believe he is two and a half years old already. I try to treasure every moment of his childhood, but it goes by so fast. I love him so I can almost hear his bones grow.

When I was little I used to catch you watching me with that funny look in your eyes like you expected me to evaporate or something. Now, I look at Lee in the same way, and I know why. It's the moments we have together that evaporate, isn't it?

Yes, Amy . . .

. . . we have this moment to hold in our hands,
And to touch as it slips through our fingers like sand;
Yesterday's gone, and tomorrow may never come,
But we have this moment, today!

Joy Comes in the Morning

If you've knelt beside the rubble
Of an aching, broken heart,
When the things you gave your life to fell apart;
You're not the first to be acquainted
With sorrow, grief, or pain,
But the Master promised sunshine after rain.

  Hold on my child,
  Joy comes in the morning,
  Weeping only lasts for the night;
  Hold on my child,
  Joy comes in the morning,
  The darkest hour means
  Dawn is just in sight.

To invest your seed of trust in God
In mountains you can't move,
You've risked your life on things you cannot prove;
But to give the things you cannot keep
For what you cannot lose
Is the way to find
The joy God has for you.

Joy Comes in the Morning

Hard times come to every person. Until the grip of this old world is forever broken by that final blast from Michael's trumpet, we will go on having what one hymn writer called "the night seasons" here on earth. No one is exempt from heartache. But the night cannot last forever, and the darkest hour is just before the dawn. God has promised that "weeping may endure for a night, but joy cometh in the morning" (Ps. 30:5 KJV).

One night while driving, Bill and I were listening to an African-American pastor on the radio encouraging his congregation — as well as his radio audience. With a heartfelt genuine compassion for his people, he kept repeating this promise from Psalm 30: "Weeping endures for the night!" he would say, asking them to repeat the words after him.

"But joy comes in the morning! Let me hear you, now. Weeping endures for the night...." The people would sing that phrase back to him.

"But *joy* comes in the morning!" With one great voice they returned the affirmation. "Joy comes in the morning!"

Eventually the organ punctuated the truth. Its great music swelled like waves cresting on the beach. "Joy, joy comes in the morning!"

As we listened, the problems in our own lives seemed to settle into perspective in the immense power of God and His great faithfulness since the psalmist first wrote the words: "Weeping may endure for a night, but joy cometh in the morning"!

The song that resulted from that experience has spoken to us for more than twenty years and has been used by God to give perspective and encouragement to many who have written to us or spoken to us at concerts. Over the years we have come to understand that pain is, as C. S. Lewis once called it, "God's megaphone." It is a useful tool in the hand of the Master Craftsman of our souls to hollow out spaces in us for holding the joy in the morning!

When the hard times of life come, we know that no matter how tragic the circumstances seem, no matter how long the spiritual drought, no matter how long and dark the days, the sun is sure to break through; the dawn will come. The warmth of His assurance will hold us in an embrace once again, and we will know that our God has been there all along. We will hear Him say, through it all, "Hold on, my child, joy comes in the morning!"

That's Worth Everything

Some men will trade the warmth of home and friends
For just a taste of fame;
Some men will risk their reputations
That men may know their name;
But just to know that all is clear between
My soul and God's dear Son,
And hear Him say, "Well done,"
Oh, that's worth ev'rything.

Just to know the future's His forever,
Just to feel the freedom of a child;
Just to know the past is gone and sunshine's here to stay,
And He is Lord of all,
Oh, that's worth everything.

To know when tiny feet walk in the path that I have left behind,
That they will make their way to Jesus,
Contentment there to find;
And just to know down deep within my heart
That I have wronged no man,
To fit my Master's plan,
Oh, that's worth ev'rything

Just to know the future's His forever,
Just to feel the freedom of a child;
Just to know the past is gone and sunshine's here to stay,
And He is Lord of all,
Oh, that's worth everything.

That's Worth Everything

I have heard a statement credited to a great theologian that went something like this: "The longer I live, I find I am believing fewer and fewer things, but believing them with greater and greater intensity." Bill and I have quoted that statement so often because it has become so true in our own lives.

As new believers, it seems we have rigid ideas about everything. We are often very quick to make rules for others, to have ready prescriptions for what "they" ought to do. Sometimes we're very hard on ourselves, too, and feel as if every failure is fatal.

How beautiful it is to learn that grace isn't fragile, and that in the family of God we can fail and not be a failure. We begin to learn that the particular path God leads us along is tailored for our personal growth in Him and that He can lead others, too. What a freeing relief it is to discover that we are not responsible for someone else's growth, but are only called to love, encourage, and be fellow pilgrims along this journey.

We learn that there are fewer absolutes than we once thought, but that those absolutes are more absolutely worth dying for than we ever could have imagined.

Bill and I have never been very attracted to "playing it safe" with life. A life worth living should be one of reckless abandonment to something worth abandoning oneself to. Bill says it this way: "I'm more than halfway through this life, so I should be more than half used up. And if I'm not, then what in the world am I saving myself for?" Perhaps the most important and all-encompassing words Jesus said are these: "Whoever would save his life will lose it, and whoever loses his life for my sake will find it" (Matt. 16:25 RSV).

Not long ago we sat down to make a list of those things that were, at this stage of our lives, worth everything. Our list was very short.

This list became a song we called simply "That's Worth Everything." We have discussed this list in our family and applied it in many ways. Our daughter wanted Bill to sing this song at her wedding as she started a new home with the man with whom she had chosen to spend her life. I don't know how Bill got through the song, but somehow he did.

When trying to prioritize our time and energies, it has been helpful for all of us to ask ourselves and each other, "Will it last forever? Does it have any eternity in it?" Or the way I phrase it for myself is: "Think 'forever!'" People are "forever." Relationships are "forever." God's Word will endure "forever." But the "forever" list is short indeed.

When Bill and I breathe our last breath and leave behind whatever we have done with our days, I hope this epitaph will ring true: "They gave themselves away for things that last forever." If that could be the case, then the "eternity" we've recognized and embraced here will simply open into the eternity we will embrace there, and we will be "at home" in the familiar presence of Him who is Alpha and Omega, the Beginning and the Ending, the First and the Last. And that will be worth everything.

These Are They

Oceans give up all the dead that are in them;
The graves open wide to set captives free.
And those who are roaming the earth rise to meet them —
Abraham's seed as the sands of the sea!

Like a strong, mighty army, their voices are ringing
The great cloud of witnesses sings freedom's song,
As they enter the country built by their own Father —
The promised homeland they've looked for so long.

All the strangers and pilgrims are no longer strangers;
The tired, weary wanderers wander no more.
The table is spread for the great celebration,
And the "Welcome Home!" banner flies over the door.

Oh, these are they who have come out of great tribulation
And have washed their robes in the blood of the Lamb —
They have come through deep sorrow into great jubilation;
They're redeemed by the blood of the Lamb.

These Are They

Most of us are doers. We have been conditioned since child-hood to achieve, to perform a task well, to get things done. In our society men, especially, are measured by what they accomplish. The very identity of men is all too often defined by what they do.

When two men sit down next to each other in a plane, it seems the first question they ask each other is, "What do you do?"

Women, too, seem to evaluate their worth in terms of the number of items they have checked off their to-do list. I can barely remember life before sticky notes. I have them everywhere — on the steering wheel of the car, the refrigerator, the kitchen door, the bathroom mirror — reminding me that I must "do something" to solve a problem or nurture a relationship.

In our spiritual lives, too, we are driven to *do* something: pray more, read more Scripture and devotional books, attend more retreats, join more Bible study groups. If God wants something done, we're ready to do it.

But for most of us the hardest thing God could ask us to do is to wait. I'm not very good at that. Bill is even worse. Waiting is hard.

Yet when we read of the great biblical leaders, we see that it was not uncommon for God to ask them to wait, not just a day or two, but for years until God was ready for them to act. Moses waited in Midian until in the process of time God could trust him with a burning bush experience, sending him to lead the Israelites out of bondage.

Joseph, sold into slavery by his brothers, sat for years in an Egyptian jail. There he waited until God brought circumstances together to elevate Joseph to a place of responsibility second only to the great Pharaoh. As for his relationship with his family, Joseph longed for restoration. But he had to wait almost ten years until they were ready and God had prepared their hearts.

God spoke to Abraham, telling him to leave his father's house and go to a land that He would show him. "And I will make of thee a great nation," said God, "and I will bless thee, and make thy name great; and thou shalt be a blessing."

So Abraham did what God said. That was the easy part, the *do* part. The hard part was the waiting. Abraham and Sarah believed God, so they waited for the son of the promise. And they waited. And they waited. As the years dragged on with no son, they wondered if they had heard God right. Maybe they should do something. Perhaps Abraham should sire a child by their house maid Hagar, and in that way "help God out" by using a surrogate mother. There must have been nights when Abraham said to himself, *Did I dream this promise? Was I having delusions of grandeur?*

God took Abraham for a walk out under the desert sky. Those were the days before light pollution. The velvet sky was spangled with stars so bright they seemed to be coming from some great light shining through tiny holes in a black canvas. "Count them," God said to Abraham. "Count the stars." Abraham managed to utter, more like a question than an answer, "There are too many stars to count."

"So shall thy seed be, Abraham."

God and Abraham walked by the seashore.

"Count them, Abraham. Count the grains of sand," God said.

Abraham was overwhelmed. "I can't count them," he whispered. "No man can count the grains of sand."

"So shall thy seed be."

Abraham was left alone to consider a promise made long before. Now he was old and Sarah was beyond childbearing years. . . .

I can't wait to be there to see it, can you? Old father Abraham, resting on the bosom of God, is leaning out over the battlements of glory to better focus on what looks like a huge cloud moving toward them. As he looks closer he sees not a cloud at all, but a huge marching throng stretching as far as the eye can see. Leading the procession are thousands of people clad in white robes that shine like the stars.

"Count them," God says to Abraham.

"I can't count them, Lord; there are too many. No man could count them. Who are they?"

"They are your seed, Abraham. They are the promise I made to you."

"And those in white. Who are they?"

"These are they which came out of great tribulation, and have washed their robes, and made them white in the blood of the Lamb. . . . They shall hunger no more, neither thirst any more . . . and God shall wipe away all tears from their eyes."

No matter what we are going through, no matter how long the waiting for answers, of one thing we may be sure. God is faithful. He keeps His promises. What He starts, He finishes . . . including His perfect work in us!

I Am Loved

All I had to bring were imperfections;
There was so much more I lacked than I possessed.
I could hardly comprehend His offer:
I'd bring what I had, He'd bring the rest.

I said, "If You knew, You wouldn't want me;
My scars are hidden by this face I wear."
He said, "My child, My scars go deeper;
It was love for you that put them there."

Forgiven — I repeat it — I'm forgiven!
Clean before my Lord I freely stand.
Forgiven, I can dare forgive my brother;
Forgiven, I reach out to take your hand.

   I am loved!
   I am loved!
   I can risk loving you,
   For the One who knows me best
   Loves me most.
   I am loved,
   You are loved,
   Won't you please take my hand?
   We are free to love each other,
   We are loved.

I Am Loved

"Jesus loves me, this I know, for the Bible tells me so. . . ." We sing it almost before we can walk. Preachers preach it, parents teach it, TV evangelists tell us, "God loves you!"

The most memorized verse in the Bible is probably John 3:16: "For God so loved the world, that he gave his only begotten Son . . ." (KJV). As children we learn to quote it. Yet the world seems to be dying from love starvation. Few of us seem to be able to internalize this simple truth: Jesus loves me. God's book is full of love stories that tell me so. An old rugged cross tells me so. Yet when we can't seem to love ourselves, it is hard for us to believe that anyone else could love us, especially if that Someone knows all there is to know about us.

The summer before Bill and I were married, I went home to Battle Creek, Michigan, to work at Kellogg's to earn enough money to return to Anderson University that fall. On weekends Bill would drive up to see me. When I got out of work at midnight on Friday, he would be waiting for me in the Kellogg's parking lot. I'd come out in my ugly green uniform, a few corn flakes still stuck in my hair, and climb into his red convertible. One night when I came out, he handed me an engagement ring. It wasn't much of a ring, because he didn't much like diamonds. But I wanted a ring so my friends in Michigan could see that we were engaged.

When we got married in December, he gave me the matching wedding band, but he never liked these rings. He would always say something like, "Those are the dumbest looking rings! Now, what I really like is a plain gold band. A plain band looks so . . . *married.*"

One evening, after we'd been married two or three years, we were at Kmart. Bill went to the recording department, as he always did, while I shopped for what we needed. That night I saw they were selling plain gold bands at the jewelry counter for $13.95 . . . a "blue-light special." (That was a long time ago!) I had some grocery money left, so I bought a plain gold band, took off my other rings, and put the band on my finger. I didn't say anything about it until we got to the car.

Bill pulled out his new recording and said, "How do you like this?"

"Fine," I answered. "How do you like this?" and held up my hand with the plain gold ring on my finger.

"I like that!" he said. "It just looks so married."

So, for seventeen years I wore the plain gold band I bought myself at Kmart for $13.95. (I don't even know if that's legal!)

In 1982, our group took a trip to the Holy Land just after Thanksgiving. The next February, one night when our family sat down for supper, instead of praying the blessing on our food, Bill said, "I want everybody to be quiet. I have a presentation to make." He took out a small blue box and handed it to me. I opened it and found inside a most unusual gold ring with Hebrew writing engraved around it.

"I had that made for you in Jerusalem," Bill said. "It is eighteen-karat gold and says, 'Arise, my love, and come away,' from the Song of Solomon."

I couldn't believe it! He had thought of this all on his own. He even paid for it! Of course, I don't read Hebrew. It could say, "Go away, my love," for all I know. Or it could say, "Kmart."

But I believe him and I love my ring. I put it right on and have worn it ever since. Now, he didn't say I had to wear it. I could have said, "I can't believe you really want me to have this ring." Or, "I don't know what you're trying to pull. I paid $13.95 for this ring on my finger, and you're not going to get me to take it off. No, siree!"

But that would have been crazy, don't you think? Especially when I had an 18-k gold, hand-engraved invitation to be loved by this wonderful man who knows me pretty well. He knows all my failures and my shortcomings. He knows what I can and cannot do. He knows all my bulges and figure flaws . . . and he loves me anyway.

And Jesus says to us, "I come that you might know life abundant." He wrote His love in His own blood on a cross. Then we say, "What will I have to give up?" We hang on to our little Kmart lives; we're so suspicious, so fearful of letting go, while He holds out His arms and invites us to share in His "unsearchable riches."

If only we could all believe that it isn't about our being worthy. It's about our being loved. If we could dare to believe that we are loved, it wouldn't matter what degrading thing anyone else had ever said to chip away at our self-esteem or to tear down our sense of worth. If we are loved, if we are valued by the God of the universe Himself, no one else's opinion matters. Being loved by Him whose opinion matters most gives us the security to risk loving, too, even loving ourselves.

Think of the hardest person to love you know, the most difficult person in your life. You can just count on it: That is a person who doesn't feel loved. That is the person who most needs to be loved. Bill and I have talked about this concept a great deal. It has helped us to be more long-suffering with others and more courageous about being honest about our own flaws and weaknesses.

The second verse of this song came from my own feelings of inadequacies, especially in the area of singing. It seemed ironic to me that I would spend thirty years of my life doing the thing about which I felt most insecure. Speaking, writing, teaching — these were natural ways for me to serve and, ultimately, God has given all of these back to me. But first He asked me to communicate His message through singing, and that was hard. I sometimes argued with God about it. I would ask why He didn't let me do what I was good at, what was easy for me. But I had to learn that His call is not based on our comfort zones. It's based on trusting what He is accomplishing in us.

I have come to recognize that He never asks us to do anything He has not already done. He never takes us anyplace where He has not been ahead of us. What He is after is not performance but relationship with us.

All I had to bring were imperfections;
There was so much more I lacked than I possessed.
I could hardly comprehend His offer:
I'd bring what I had; He'd bring the rest.

I said, "If You knew, You wouldn't want me;
My scars are hidden by this face I wear."
He said, "My child, My scars go deeper;
It was love for you that put them there."

I am loved!
I am loved!
I can risk loving you,
For the One who knows me best
Loves me most.
I am loved,
You are loved,
Won't you please take my hand?
We are free to love each other,
We are loved.

Go Ask

Don't ask me to explain to you how one could start again —
How hardened hearts could soften like a child.
Don't ask me how to reason out the mysteries of life,
Or how to face its problems with a smile.

   Go ask the man who's found the way
   Through tangled roads back home to stay
   When all communications were destroyed.
   Go ask the child who's walking now
   Who once was crippled, then somehow
   Her useless legs were made to jump for joy.
   Go ask the one whose burned-out mind
   Has been restored — I think you'll find
   The questions not important as before.
   Don't ask me if He's good or bad;
   I only know the guilt I had is gone,
   And I can't tell you any more.

Don't ask me how to prove to you why I know God is there.
And how I know that He could care for you.
Don't ask me why Someone so great would choose to walk with me
And trade my broken life for one that's new.

   Go ask the child who's got a dad
   To love away the hurt he had
   Before this man called Jesus touched their lives.
   Go ask the one whose fears have fled,
   Whose churning heart was quieted
   When Someone whispered "peace" to all her strife.
   Go ask the man to tell you more
   Whose life was just a raging war
   Inside himself until the Savior came.
   I don't pretend to be so wise;
   I only know He touched my eyes
   And nothing else will ever be the same!

Go Ask

There are no test tubes for proving the things of the spirit. "The proof" is lived out in a person changed by the touch of God. Debate and logic, theorizing and philosophizing can help us sort out our thoughts about life and form them into axioms and rules to live by, but the laboratory for testing those theories is life — real days stacked into years of practicing.

Bill's father, who has lived eight decades, says, "People change, but not much." I'm coming to believe that in one way he's right. Only a force greater than ourselves can change the heart and reshape the human personality. And yet the tough circumstances of life can be tools, when used by the Master, to shape us into something far more beautiful than we could ever have dreamed.

Deep life changes wrought by God begin with a change in direction. Something comes to slow us down and stop us — a crisis, a tragedy, a failure, a gnawing dissatisfaction — something that makes us realize we are totally inadequate to run our lives, something that makes us admit that if we keep going the way we're going, we will self-destruct or live out our days in dull mediocrity. This "stop down" makes us realize we are helpless to "fix things," to change on our own. Whatever gets our attention and causes us to call out to God is a gift to our lives, no matter how hard the halt "throws" us at the time.

This "turning around" has been called by many names: conversion, salvation, finding God. Whatever it is named, it is necessary to bring us from living a pattern out of harmony with the God of the universe and into alignment with God's patterns and rhythms of love and grace.

After this turning point, change seems to be gradual, especially to the person who is changing — being molded into the likeness of God's Son, but feeling less than adequate, less than holy, much less than perfect. Before this process, we may have felt arrogant and self-sufficient, but now this is a humbling experience that paradoxically brings peace because we sense our life is becoming more in harmony with the Holy Spirit who now lives in us. We come to realize the work is something He is doing in us, and our job is to surrender to that amazing work.

Bill and I have often talked about this process, not only in others but in ourselves and in each other. We've discussed it most when we are most discouraged with our own progress. But, as we noted in the song we thought we were writing for kids, *We are a promise* God made, an infinite possibility, and He will keep His promise to the world and to Himself; what He has begun in us He will be faithful to finish.

The story of the blind man healed by Jesus continues to surface in our writing because it's so refocusing. We can't always explain the theological intricacies of what God is doing or has done in us. We may not have chosen the route God brought us. I may not understand what God is up to in you — or you may not recognize what He's doing in me. Like the blind man, I make a simple claim: "All I know is that once I was blind and now I see." Sighted eyes are enough. Hearing ears are enough.

This simple song is made up of the stories of real people changed by a real God. If it has power, it is because there is power in the irrefutable proof of God at work in human lives: formerly crippled legs that now can walk; daddies that were gone — physically, spiritually, emotionally — now returned home and engaged in the lives of their children; minds that were fried by drugs, now restored and lucid. For proof? Go ask anyone who's being changed by the hand of Jesus. I am one who is, even as I write this, being changed into the image of my Master and Friend. I'm not what I want to be. I'm not what I'm going to be. But, thank God, I'm not what I was! (But that's another song!)

> And they overcame him [the accuser] by the blood of the Lamb, and by the word of their testimony (Rev. 12:11 KJV).

We Are So Blessed

We are so blessed by the gifts from Your hand —
We just can't understand
Why You loved us so much.
We are so blessed!
We just can't find a way
Or the words that can say
Thank You, Lord, for Your touch.

When we're empty, You fill us 'til we overflow!
And when we're hungry, You feed us
And cause us to know. . . .

We are so blessed!
Take what we have to bring —
Take it all — everything!
Lord, we bring it to You.

We are so blessed by the gifts from Your hand,
We just can't understand
Why You loved us so much.
We are so blessed!
We just can't find a way
Or the words that can say
Thank You, Lord, for Your touch.

We just want to say
Lord, we love You so much.

We Are So Blessed

There is something about harvest time in Indiana that makes me feel that I should finish something. Perhaps it is the threshing machines cleaning up the rows of wheat and spitting the swollen ripe kernels into the waiting grain trucks to be taken off to storage bins in preparation for winter. Maybe it is the wide plows that turn the traces of cornstalks and dry soybean plants under, leaving the fresh black earth like a velvet carpet laid in neat squares alongside the green-sprouted fields of winter wheat. Or it could be the squirrels skittering around the yard stuffing acorns and walnuts in their jaws, then racing off to bury their treasure. Or maybe it's the last of the apple crop being pressed into fragrant cider or baked with cinnamon and brown sugar before the frost.

Whatever the reason, this is the season to finish things, to tie up loose ends, to save and store, to harvest and be sure there is enough of everything that matters to last us through the hard times.

And how does one finish a season of the heart? How can we harvest and store the bounty of the spirit and save the fruits we cannot see? Gratitude is the instrument of harvest. It ties the golden sheaves in bundles; it plucks the swollen kernels in great round bales. It picks the crimson fruit and digs the rounded root that sometimes has made the difference between life and death of relationships.

Let's be thankful!

Thankful for plenty — plenty and more — of things to eat and wear; of shelter and warmth; of beauty, such as art and colors and textures; of means of transportation, such as cars, bikes, vans, buses, planes . . . and feet. Plenty of things that money can't buy, such as tenderness and inspiration and revelation and insight . . . books, words, songs, discussions.

Thankful for health — health that we take so for granted that we schedule our lives, assuming always that everything will be normal,

> that legs will walk . . . to school, to work, to play;
>
> that eyes will see . . . to read, to experience, to learn;
>
> that ears will hear . . . the music, the instructions, the warnings, the blessings, the sounds of nature;
>
> that bodies will function . . . that food will digest, energy will be generated to perform our daily tasks;
>
> that minds will comprehend . . . the beauty, the concepts and ideas, the dangers, the failures;
>
> that hands will work . . . to reach, to hug, to write, to drive, to rake leaves and sweep floors, to fold clothes and play instruments — pianos, flutes, violins, drums, oboes.

Thankful for family — family with individual personalities, gifts, needs, and dreams, each such a gift. Family immediate and family extended, all feeding into what we are and what we will become. Even family departed, those who have lived out their part and left their heritage of hard work, integrity, grit, love, tenderness, faith, humor.

Thankful for friends — for stimulating, vivacious, provoking, comforting, disturbing, encouraging, agitating, blessing, loving, warming, forgiving friends.

Thankful for hope and love — hope and love, a deep assurance that God is in control of our lives, an assurance that is not threatened by fear of nuclear annihilation, national economic failure, personal physical disability, or even death.

Thankful for children — children who give us new eyes to see, new ears to hear, new hands to touch, new minds to understand ... all the old things.

And thankful for courage — the courage to go on trusting people, risking love, daring to believe in what could be, all because of the confirming experience of daily trusting God and finding Him utterly trustworthy.

And, because the seasons are built into the very fiber of our being, thank God for harvest time, a time for finishing what's been started, a time to be aware, to take account, and to realize the life we've been given.

Because God has promised that if we harvest well with the tools of thanksgiving, there will be seeds for planting in the spring.

Fully Alive

Don't let me miss all the glory around me
Waiting for heaven someday to come;
Open my eyes to miraculous Mondays,
And make my feet march to eternity's drum.

> Fully alive in Your Spirit;
> Lord, make me fully alive!
> Fully aware of Your presence, Lord,
> Totally, fully alive!

Don't let me wait for some far-off forever
To say what I feel to the ones I hold dear,
Risking the pain and the joys of loving,
Keep me awake and alive while I'm here!

Help me to see in this moment my calling;
Don't let me wait for some "field far away."
Cries in my street, lives that are broken —
Lord, let me see them and touch them . . . today!

> Fully alive in Your Spirit;
> Lord, make me fully alive!
> Fully aware of Your presence, Lord,
> Totally, fully alive!

Fully Alive

Recently, on my way to get my hair trimmed, I stopped for breakfast and a cup of hot coffee at the local pancake house. I intended to steal a moment to be alone before the day began and its many demands crowded my time and took their bite of my energies.

"Just an egg and a homemade biscuit," I told the waitress, "and a coffee, please." I handed back the menu and turned to the book I'd brought to jump-start my mind.

I had barely finished the second page before she returned with my breakfast. *Fast,* I thought. She poured the coffee and asked if there'd be anything else. "No, I'm fine, thank you," I answered, my eyes really looking into hers for the first time.

She smiled. "Enjoy!" she said, then hurried back to deliver someone else's order.

"Enjoy!"

Her final word hung in the air above my corner booth like a blessing—and more. It was a sermon of sorts. The taste of a fresh egg and a warm biscuit. The warmth of a cup of hot coffee in my hands on this Winnie-the-Pooh blustery day. The colors, the textures, the aromas, the voices, the morning music that surrounded me. "Enjoy!"

It was a choice she had offered me. I could go through this day oblivious to the miracles all around me or I could tune in and "enjoy!"

Her invitation returned again and again to bless my day. As I lay back at the shampoo bowl, I noticed the fresh green apple smell of the conditioner; I "enjoyed" the scalp message and the warm water—right from the tap—that was "blessing" my head. Two weeks earlier I had returned from a country that offered precious few faucets that mix hot and cold water to just the right temperature. I realized then that this simple convenience was a gift to my busy life.

"Mamaw!" Grandson Jesse's happy voice greeted me as I got out of the car. His strong little arms were already around my neck, and he was covering my face with the kisses he'd recently learned to aim at a chosen target. I could hear, I could feel, I could see this precious, sturdy child who blessed my days with the joy of being adored—as only an innocent child can adore. I was his "mamaw"!

I stopped by the grocery store. Bill had asked me to get him some green grapes. (We should invest in a vineyard!) The produce section of the new superstore was something to behold—a carnival of color, tastes, textures, and smells—all seeming as fresh from the earth as the moment someone had harvested them.

"Enjoy!" the waitress sang to my heart.

The phone rang. "Come out here for supper, Mom." It was our second daughter Amy who had just returned with her husband Andrew and little boy Lee from a trip to visit Andrew's parents in Birmingham. "We want to show you what we've done to the cabin." The digital telephone relayed her cheery voice as clearly as if she were standing in my kitchen.

I looked out the window above the sink at the spring rain bathing the lilac bushes and just-planted pink geraniums around the lamppost. Two pairs of cardinals darted through the grape arbor and landed on the birdbath, where they tossed water drops up to blend with the drops still falling from the sky.

"Enjoy!"

Bill came in the back door and dumped a pile of mail on the counter. "Got any soup left?" he asked, lifting the lid on the pot that simmered on the stove. He barely took a breath before he shared his excitement about the way the new video he was editing was coming together. Tears welled up in his eyes as he described how powerful the spontaneous testimonies were at our last "Homecoming Friends" filming. "God is doing something bigger than all of us," he said with awe in his voice. "We're just privileged to be at the right place at the right time to see it."

Enjoy! I thought.

As the day unfolded, moment by moment, I felt like Emily in Thorton Wilder's play "Our Town." Emily had died giving birth to her first baby. But she couldn't resign herself to death just yet, and she was granted her wish to go back to relive just one day. She was advised to pick an unimportant day, because she would not only live it, but watch herself living it; the most unimportant day of her life would be important enough. Emily chose her twelfth birthday. *Just a regular day,* she thought, *that wouldn't be too much to ask.*

But as what she thought would be a quite regular day progressed, it was the "regular" that was so poignant she could hardly bear it: the smell of coffee perking; the feeling of her young skin between the fresh clean sheets; the sight of her mother — so young — bustling about the kitchen doing the "daily" things; the visit from the awkward teen-aged boy next door who would grow up to be Emily's husband, George, the father of her baby.

Finally, she was overwhelmed by the beauty of regular life: "Oh, earth," she exclaims, "you're too wonderful for anybody to realize you."

Jesus intended for us to be overwhelmed by the blessings of regular days. He said it was the reason He had come: "I am come that they might have life, and that they might have it more abundantly" (John 10:10 KJV).

Each day, each moment is so pregnant with eternity that if we "tune in" to it, we can hardly contain the joy. I have a feeling this is what happened to Moses when he saw the burning bush. Maybe Yahweh performed laser surgery on his eyes so he could see what was always there, and Moses was just so overwhelmed with the "glory" of God that the very ground he stood on became infused with "holiness" and the bushes along the mountain path burned with splendor. Whatever happened, the burning bush experience also sharpened Moses' awareness of the pain of his people in the light of God's presence.

Bill's dad is always reminding us that "This ain't the rehearsal, kids. It's the real thing. Don't miss it while it's happening." Pain and pleasure, laughter and tears are all around us, too, if we can see them and respond to them.

Several years ago we had written a song that went through my mind again that day as I sipped my coffee and watched the rain streaming down the window: "Fully alive in Your Spirit; Lord, make me fully alive!" I'd heard a lot of sermons in my day, but the best sermon I'd heard in a long time was preached in one word by a busy waitress as she poured a cup of coffee.

God has given us this day. I don't want to miss it.

Enjoy!

Upon This Rock

When others see with earthly eyes just what they want to see,
You will see the things that never die.
You will know and recognize by simple, childlike faith
The priceless truth that others will deny.

When others say I'm just a man who liked to dream his dreams,
When others call a miracle a myth,
You'll listen for eternity in moments as they pass
And see with spirit eyes what others miss.

If in a simple carpenter you see the Son of God,
If you will choose to lose when you could win;
If you will give your life away for nothing in return,
Then you are where My kingdom will begin.

    Upon this Rock I'll build My kingdom.
    Upon this Rock forever and ever it shall stand.
    And all the pow'rs of hell itself shall nevermore prevail against it,
    For Satan's thrones are built on sinking sand.
    Upon this Rock I'll build My kingdom,
    And on this Rock forever and ever it shall stand.
    Upon this Rock of revelation I'll build a strong and mighty nation.
    And it shall stand the storms of time upon this Rock.

Upon This Rock

*J*erusalem in summer is hot and dusty. This city on a hill is surrounded by desert except for where irrigation water has been brought in by aqueduct or by more modern devices. But north of Jerusalem, through the rugged beauty of the northern kingdoms, past the Sea of Galilee, then slightly to the east, is a surprising oasis in the foothills of Mount Hermon. A natural spring gushes from the rock, then pours into a basin below. This is one water source of the Jordan River.

No wonder this cool, green place hidden in the foothills for centuries was chosen as a vacation spot for the privileged. When our family visited this place, our historian-guide explained that one of these rocks once grounded an ancient shrine to Pan, whom the Greeks believed to be the god of nature. It was here that Herod much later built his summer palace away from the dust and heat of Jerusalem. It was here, too, that the Caesars came to vacation. The city of Caesarea Philippi, close to this spot, was, many believe, named after Caesar by Herod to appease the Roman emperor.

It was likely that Jesus stopped here with His disciples after healing and teaching in the coastal cities of Tyre and Sidon, after feeding thousands in the hills above the Sea of Galilee, and tangling with the Pharisees and Sadducees in Magdala.

When Jesus came into the coasts of Caesarea Philippi, He asked His disciples, "Whom do men say that I, the Son of man, am?"

Here, where the ancient Greeks had built shrines to pagan gods on one rock, the corrupt King Herod of the Jews had built a summer house on another rock, and the head of the powerful Roman state had built a retreat on another rock, Jesus stands near the cool spring of pure water, waiting for the disciples to answer His question.

"Some say John the Baptist, others say Elijah, and others Jeremiah or one of the prophets."

Jesus makes His question personal. "But who do you say that I am?"

It is not surprising that Simon Peter blurts out an answer. What is surprising is what he says: "You are the Christ, the Son of the living God."

Jesus knows that Peter is not the discerning type, that he could not have arrived at this conclusion on the basis of his ability to be philosophical or logical or insightful. Bless him!

"Flesh and blood has not revealed this to you, but my Father who is in heaven," Jesus says looking gently at Peter. Then He uses Peter's name to make one of the most important pronouncements of His ministry on earth: "And I tell you, you are Peter [He uses the masculine for rock, *petros*], and on this rock [Jesus uses the feminine, *petra*] I will build my church, and the powers of death shall not prevail against it."

Not on the rock of the Greeks with their great knowledge and philosophies. Not on the rock of Jewish law. Not on the rock of earthly power and authority. But upon a rock that would stand after all philosophies and knowledge and religious scepters and earthly power had faded into oblivion. This kingdom would stand when all else had fallen. It would be built, not in this place where water, so vital to life in a desert land, rushed from a rock and flowed into the Jordan, but in a place unseen with the human eye. He would build His kingdom on the rock of the divine revelation of God the Father. Jesus Himself had come to be the living, walking revelation of the Father. He was the stone the builders rejected that had become the cornerstone. On this rock God would build His kingdom. It would be firmly established not north of Galilee but in the hearts of believers, no matter how simple or wise they might be. Peter would be forever an example; if Peter could receive this revelation, anyone could receive it.

On this rock of revelation, on the truth of God that Jesus had served to show, Jesus would build an unseen, living kingdom, an eternal unshakable kingdom. Armies could not march against it. Philosophies could not debate it. Powers could not destroy it. Governments, secular or religious, could not legislate it into or out of existence. It was being established not with brute force, but with love. This kingdom in the hearts of believers, brought about by the revelation of God to simple trusting hearts, would stand the storms of time.

This kingdom will one day become as visible to all as it is now invisible. And the river that gushes from this Rock will flow into a place where all the saints of all time will be refreshed and their thirst satisfied.

Many years after that day with Jesus and the disciples, the apostle John got a glimpse of what was to come. What he saw, too, was a divine revelation from God:

> And he showed me a pure river of water of life, clear as crystal, proceeding out of the throne of God and of the Lamb. In the midst of the street of it, and on either side of the river, was there the tree of life, which bare twelve manner of fruits, and yielded her fruit every month: and the leaves of the tree were for the healing of the nations. And there shall be no more curse: but the throne of God and of the Lamb shall be in it; and his servants shall serve him: And they shall see his face; and his name shall be in their foreheads. And there shall be no night there; and they need no candle, neither light of the sun; for the Lord God giveth them light: and they shall reign for ever and ever. (Rev. 22:1–5 KJV)

The Stage Is Bare

The stage is bare,
The crowds are gone;
Love we shared
Still lingers on.
We sang and played,
We laughed and cried —
And in our fumbling way we tried
To say what only hearts can know;
And all too soon we had to go.
But now here in this darkened room
Just empty seats — just me . . . and You.

It was easy to call You "Lord"
When a thousand voices sang Your praise —
But there's no one to hear me now
So hear me now . . . be near me now, I pray.

The stage is bare,
The crowds are gone;
Lord, now's the time I need Your Song
To give me joy and certainty.
When no one else is watching me,
I need You more than words can say.
Tomorrow's such a daily day —
And I so need to feel You then
Holding my hand —
Please hold me then
I need You . . . Lord.

The Stage Is Bare

The concert had been a sellout. An enthusiastic audience of all ages. Waves of laughter and applause between the music and the singing. A great night!

By the time we were finished tearing down displays in the lobby, putting equipment in the bus, and changing our clothes in the dressing room, the building was empty. All the lights were out except for one lone lightbulb dangling by a frayed cord from the ceiling above the stage. As we carried our bags across the stage to the back door, we stopped for a moment and talked about the evening. The single light and the huge silent room were such a contrast to the spotlights and the excitement of an hour ago.

"It was a great night," one of the performers said. "But the question is, do the things we sang and said then work now?"

There is always a danger that politicians will start believing their own press releases, that kids will not be able to tell fairy tales from reality, that performers and actors will not be capable of separating the stage and the floodlights from their Monday mornings and daylight.

Bill and I have spent a great deal of time with aspiring young artists, not so much to help them "make it," but in the hopes of teaching them some things that may save them from themselves when they do make it.

In our culture, talent often results in what the world would call "success," but it has been our experience that success is often much harder to deal with than failure. In fact, failure is often good for us human beings; we learn from our failures. We're often destroyed by success.

The Palm Sunday story in the Bible carries a very modern application. It's easy to praise the Lord in a crowd of cheering worshipers, singing songs and "lifting holy hands." But when the dust clears, and the music stops, and the lights are reduced to a bare lightbulb dangling from a frayed cord, what then? Is our praise as convincing when we're alone in an elevator? Does it "preach" when we're the only person in the congregation?

I once heard someone say about a Christian speaker: "I'd be more impressed if I ever heard him pray when he wasn't on stage."

My father was a pastor, and I often heard him quote 1 Corinthians 9:27, Paul's high standard, which my dad held up for himself: "But I keep under my body, and bring it into subjection: lest that by any means, when I have preached to others, I myself should be a castaway" (KJV). That verse was like a caution light that flashed over my parents' ministry. It is a caution light for me. It is a warning for Bill's and my ministry of writing and speaking and parenting and living in our little town. What we do when the stage is dark and bare is so much more important than what we do when it's bright and full.

When our traveling groups meet for a time of prayer before concerts, we have often prayed that we would be as real at McDonald's after the concert as we seem during the concert, that our lives with the stagehands and the auditorium's staff would be as convincing as our lives in front of the spotlight.

When it is all said and done, I hope our children and our parents, our neighbors, and the people with whom we work will see our praise lived out much more articulately than we are ever able to express in words and in print.

May our failures and shortcomings be redeemed by the sweet love and grace of Jesus so that His spirit makes a more lasting memory than our fragile humanity.

Broken and Spilled Out

One day a plain village woman,
Driven by love for her Lord,
Recklessly poured out a valuable essence
Disregarding the scorn.
And once it was broken and spilled out,
A fragrance filled all the room,
Like a pris'ner released from his shackles,
Like a spirit set free from the tomb.

> Broken and spilled out — just for love of You, Jesus.
> My most precious treasure, lavished on Thee;
> Broken and spilled out and poured at Your feet.
> In sweet abandon, let me be spilled out and used up for Thee.

Whatever it takes to be Yours, Lord;
Whatever it takes to be clean —
I just can't live without Your sweet approval,
No matter what it may mean!
I throw myself at Your feet, Lord,
Broken by Your love for me;
May the fragrance of total commitment
Be the only defense that I need.

Lord, You were God's precious treasure,
His loved and His own perfect Son,
Sent here to show me the love of the Father;
Yes, just for love it was done!
And though You were perfect and holy,
You gave up Yourself willingly;
And You spared no expense for my pardon —
You were spilled out and wasted for me!

> Broken and spilled out — just for love of me, Jesus.
> God's most precious treasure, lavished on me;
> You were broken and spilled out and poured at my feet.
> In sweet abandon, Lord, You were spilled out and used up for me.

Broken and Spilled Out

The pressure to produce is a constant companion of writers and artists. The consuming public is fickle. A novelist is only as valuable as his or her latest book; a singer is measured by the success of the latest release and how many songs "charted." Painters and sculptors are always pulled between creating pieces that express their souls and compromising their creative skills to comply with the current trend that "sells" or conforms to the most influential new school of criticism.

Many young recording artists have started out with a heart full of inspiration and a passion to communicate a message in a style unique to them, only to be told by some record company or agent that they must dilute their message, revamp their style, and reshape their image. Few are mature or financially confident enough to withstand the implied threats not to "re-sign" them to the label if they refuse the "expertise" of those who "know the market."

One day on the bus, traveling to a concert, Steve Green and I were talking about the pressure to produce. While feeling frustrated by his busy schedule and the expectations to create a new solo project that could get "radio play," he was also exhilarated by the part-time jobs he and Marijean had, working with the youth of a local church. He wanted to record and sing songs that would relate to the lives and problems of these teenagers and their parents, whether or not the songs worked for hit-driven radio.

As for my frustration: I was feeling a need to write without the pressure of a deadline. I wanted to create what was in my heart without regard to its sales potential in the current Christian market. I had recently gone off to a cabin in the woods where I write and, at the end of two days, I had written only some personal poetry and entries in my journal. I had read, walked in the woods, talked to God and, in general, restored my soul. What a rich time! But when I returned home, I couldn't help feeling guilty for having to tell Bill I hadn't moved ahead on projects we had committed to or finished songs we had started!

Steve listened to me and then told about the Wednesday night prayer meeting the week before at their local church. "Marijean stood up, so moved by the presence of the Lord, and talked about her deep hunger and thirst to really know Christ in His fullness," Steve said. "She confessed some faults and asked the people to pray for her that nothing would stand in the way of a pure and intimate relationship with Jesus. It broke our church apart. In her sweet honesty, she was able to minister in a way I seldom can."

We talked about what amazing things God does when we can totally get out of the way and love Him with the innocence and abandonment of a child.

"What would happen," I wondered, "if I wrote my very best poetry for no one but Jesus? I long to give Him the very best ... knowing it will never be published ... lift my gift like a burning incense to Him alone."

"And how I long," Steve said, "to be able to give God my best performance as if no one could hear but Him."

We talked about Marijean's brokenness and how, like Mary who broke the perfume vessel to bathe Jesus' feet in its precious contents, Marijean had through her vulnerability bathed the church in the sweet fragrance of her pure hunger to serve God alone.

"Write me a song about that," Steve said. "I'd like to record a song that would always remind me what my ministry should be — an irresistible fragrance that can come only from a vessel broken."

He went back to talk with the others on the bus. I found a yellow tablet and began to write. The lyric that resulted was "Broken and Spilled Out." It moved me. I wanted the music for it to capture the deep longing to give Jesus the best part, the most perfect offering of the heart.

Bill George, an outstanding keyboard artist, set the lyrics to music, and Steve recorded the song.

It has been a very special song for me. It constantly reminds me that only a love that has no regard for vessels and jars — appearances or image — only a love that will lavish its most treasured essence on the feet of Jesus can produce the kind of fragrance that draws cynics and believers alike into His presence.

Praise You

(Psalm 139)

There's no place where You're not there;
I'll never drift from Your love and care.
There's not a thing about me that You don't know.
The wings of the morning
Will take me to You;
The blackness of night,
Your light will shine through;
You're already there
No matter where I may go.
Even before I came to be,
Your loving eyes were looking at me —
You're even closer, closer than the breath I take.
Mother and father,
More than a friend to me,
Beginning and ending
And living of life to me,
The song I find myself singing when I awake.

So I will praise You! / Lord, I praise You!
Now I praise You / For bearing me up
And giving me wings, / For lifting my sights
To heavenly things, / For being the songs
I can't help but sing — / Praise You!

Look at me, Lord, I'm open to You.
Do anything that You want to do —
You know me even better than I know myself.
I'll not be afraid
Of what You can see
'Cause You know the person
Inside of me;
I won't even try
To hide what You know so well.
Lord, just be patient with my mistakes;
I want to be Yours whatever it takes.
I've learned that life without You is no life at all,
Failures and talents
And schemes I bring to You;
Aspirations and dreams
I sing to You —
I'll just be here ready
Whenever You call.

So I will praise You!
Lord, I praise You!
Now I praise You
For bearing me up
And giving me wings,
For lifting my sights
To heavenly things,
For being the songs
I can't help but sing —
Praise You!

Praise You

*I*t was the year we wrote the musical *Kids Under Construction.* We decided to travel to Puerto Rico to combine a vacation with some work time with Ron Huff — conceive the musical, create the staging, and lay out the plot. Ron and Donna, our whole family, and my mother spent a week on a lovely beach lined by palm trees and tropical flowers.

Our eight-year-old Amy thought Donna Huff was the most beautiful woman she'd ever seen. To imitate her, Amy would pick fresh hibiscus blossoms to pin in her hair each evening. Benjy, a year younger, caught lizards by the tail and collected sand crabs in his plastic pail. Suzanne, at twelve, teetered between childhood and womanhood. One minute she was chasing lizards or building sand castles with Benjy; the next she was writing postcards to a boy back home.

We all knew how priceless these moments were; we memorized the sunsets, absorbed the music of the birds, and pressed exotic flowers between the pages of the books we'd brought to read.

As for our work, we all wrote and talked about ideas, great and small, and used the welcome break to refresh our spirits.

One day while the children played at the water's edge with my mother (who was always the biggest "kid" of all), Bill and I took a walk down the beach. It was easy to walk a long way and not think about how far you'd gone. When we realized how long we'd been away, we turned back toward the hotel. We were still quite a distance away when we saw a child running toward us, waving his arms. Soon we realized it was Benjy, urgently trying to tell us something. We ran to meet him.

"Suzanne lost her glasses in the ocean!" he yelled over the thunder of the surf. "She was picking up shells and a big wave came in and knocked off her glasses. The tide washed them out to sea!"

"How long ago?" I asked, thinking about how quickly these strong currents had been carrying things — even children — down the beach.

"About fifteen minutes ago. We've been looking for them ever since."

My mind raced. A coral reef ran parallel to the shoreline about a hundred feet out. There were urgent warnings of an undertow — "Strong Currents." Objects like sand toys or rafts caught by a wave had been carried down the beach as fast as the children could run to catch them.

By now we were shouting back and forth to Suzanne. "Where did you lose them?" I yelled.

"Right here. I was standing right here!"

She was knee-deep in water as the tide was coming in. "I can't see a thing, Mother. What are we going to do?"

"Let's pray," I said and I took her two hands in mine.

Then I thought to myself, *What are you doing? You're going to ruin this kid's faith. Those glasses have long since been pulled out to sea by the undertow, most likely smashed to bits against the coral reef. If we even find any pieces, they will have washed ashore far down the beach!* But I was too far into this to turn back. Holding Suzanne's hands and standing knee-deep in water, I prayed: "Jesus, You know how much Suzanne needs her glasses, and that we are far from home and know no doctors to have them replaced here. We are Your children and this is Your ocean. You know where the glasses are, so we're asking You to send them back."

Just then Suzanne squeezed my hand and interrupted my prayer. "Mother! Something just hit my leg!" She let go of my hand, reached down into the water, and pulled out her glasses. They were in one piece and not even scratched!

We danced a jig of praise and she ran off to tell the others who were searching farther down the beach.

Much later that evening, after we'd had our dinner and the kids were ready for bed, I took out the Bible and opened it to Psalms to read something that might fit the sounds of the surf pounding the shore outside our room's open patio doors. I chose a psalm we'd read many times, but never had we heard it as we did that night.

O Lord, you have examined my heart and know everything about me. You know when I sit or stand. When far away you know my every thought. You chart the path ahead of me and tell me where to stop and rest. Every moment, you know where I am. You know what I am going to say before I even say it. You both precede and follow me, and place your hand of blessing on my head. This is too glorious, too wonderful to believe! I can *never* be lost to your Spirit! I can *never* get away from my God! If I go up to heaven, you are there; if I go down to the place of the dead, you are there. If I ride the morning winds to the farthest oceans, even there your hand will guide me, your strength will support me. (Ps. 139:1–10 LB)

When we had finished all of Psalm 139, we could hardly believe that God's Word had been so specific for us . . . so familiar yet as new and fresh as this day's miracle. Together we thanked God that He is a God who chose to be involved in our lives, that truly He had scheduled our days; we marveled at the truth that we couldn't even "count how many times a day His thoughts turned toward us."

Psalm 139 has "returned" many times to visit our family. Our children are now reading it to their children. Soon after that trip Bill and I wrote the psalm into a song we called "Praise You." It has been arranged for choirs and recorded by various artists. But it will always be for us a reminder of the day a little girl prayed with her mother on an island beach for a pair of glasses lost at sea.

I've Just Seen Jesus

We knew He was dead.
"It is finished," He'd said;
We had watched as His life ebbed away.
Then we all stood around
'Til guards took Him down —
Joseph begged for His body that day.
It was late afternoon
When we got to the tomb,
Wrapped His body in and sealed up the grave.
So I know how you feel —
His death was so real —
But please listen and hear what I say:

> I've just seen Jesus! I tell you He's alive!
> I've just seen Jesus! My precious Lord . . . alive!
> And I knew, He really saw me too! — as if 'til now, I'd never lived!
> All that I've done before won't matter anymore —
> I've just seen Jesus! I've just seen Jesus!
> I will never be the same again.

It was just before dawn —
I was running along
Barely able to see where to go —
For the tears in my eyes
And the dusky sunrise
Seemed to cloud up my vision so.
It was His voice I first heard —
Those kind gentle words
Asking what was my reason for tears.
And I sobbed in despair,
"My Lord is not there!"
He said, "Child! It is I. I am here!"

I've Just Seen Jesus

Many epic films have been made of biblical stories and the life of Christ — *The Ten Commandments, Ben Hur, Jesus of Nazareth,* and *Quo Vadis,* to name a few. Hollywood effects have made the Red Sea part and the waves form a giant wall of water for the cast of thousands to march to freedom from Pharaoh's army. Technology has caused a river to turn to blood and leprosy to disappear.

But for me no film device has been as powerful as that used in the old black and white Cecil B. DeMille film *King of Kings.* Instead of casting an actor to portray Christ, the director chose to show only Jesus' feet walking along the way. The cameras focused not on Jesus but on the faces of those who were affected by Him. Made before the days of "talking films," the movie forced its audience to read on the screen what Jesus said, and then see the result of His words in the lives changed or the bodies healed.

I was a small child when I saw this film, yet I can remember scenes in detail: the face of the woman taken in adultery when her eyes met the Master; the way the crippled child looked when he felt strength flowing into his withered leg; the joy the ten lepers expressed when they peeled off the bandages that had held their rotting skin on their bones.

But movie depictions would pale in the reality of walking with the living Christ. What an experience it would have been to see Jesus as He walked the dusty streets of Nazareth, to sit near Him on the grassy slopes of Galilee and with our own ears hear Him say, "Blessed are the poor in spirit, for theirs is the kingdom of heaven. . . . Blessed are the meek, for they will inherit the earth." To have Him take me by the hand and raise me to my feet as He spoke the words, "Neither do I condemn you; go and sin no more." To have Him touch our dead child and say, "She is only sleeping. Child, get up." What an experience it would have been to say at the dinner table after such a day, "We've just seen this Jesus!"

But of all the encounters with the living, walking Christ of history, none would have been as amazing as those the disciples who loved Him best experienced the third day after the crucifixion. Mary Magdalene, Mary the mother of Jesus, Martha and Mary of Bethany, Peter, John, Thomas . . . on Friday they had stood at the foot of the cross. Every unbearable moment of that afternoon had been etched in their memory: the nails, the thud of the cross as it dropped into the hole the executioners had dug for it, the seven times Jesus had groaned out His last words. How could they ever forget the ugly, taunting remarks of the Romans? The contrast between the curses of one thief who died beside Him and the plea of another whose eyes met Jesus' as He promised that that very day they would be together in paradise — these memories played back over and over again as these witnesses tried to sleep that Saturday night.

They had waited around — through the storm, through the eerie blackness of midday until evening when the soldiers came to confirm that the bodies were lifeless. It hadn't been hard to take Jesus' body down from the cross; the nails — from the rough treatment and the weight of His body — had torn large holes through His hands.

Joseph of Arimathea spoke to the soldiers and asked for permission to take Jesus' body for burial in an unused grave on his property. By the time the body had been released and they'd carried it to the tomb, they had little time left before sundown, the beginning of Sabbath, to wash and wrap the body. There was no doubt that Jesus was dead. The gaping wounds, especially from the spear the soldiers had jabbed in His side, had released so much blood and body fluids that He looked shrunken and dehydrated.

How tenderly they must have washed His body, His words still echoing through their minds: "Take, eat; this is my body that is broken for you." The night before they had thought that the bread and the wine and His words were only symbols as ancient as Moses. Now they realized this was a new thing — this breaking of bread He had asked them to "do in remembrance" of Him. For His part, it was no symbol. His real body here in their hands was torn to pieces. For them, too, it would become more than a symbol; it would become a call to follow His example, even if it meant losing their lives.

That Sabbath eve they had gone their separate ways in silence. There was nothing to say. It seemed to be all over. They had walked an

189

amazing journey with Him toward a promised kingdom that now seemed to lie shattered at their feet. Yet something unexplainable in their bones felt not like an end but a beginning. Perhaps they were in denial, yet there was a sense of hope in all the black hopelessness that no one could articulate — not to each other, not to themselves.

They would each tell a very personal account of those hours, for knowing Him was a personal experience, shared, yet uniquely their own. One thing for certain: No one could really see Him, or be seen by those eyes that seemed to look into one's very soul, and ever be the same again.

Then, on that Easter morning, they found the tomb empty. Mary Magdelene had actually spoken to the living Christ, and they — Peter and John — ran to check out her story. Could it be true? They felt the gamut of emotions as they entered the garden of the tomb. They could see at once the open grave, the stone leaning to one side as if it had been shoved like a child's toy out of someone's way. And then they saw the figure clothed in white, sitting on the grave slab at the foot of where they had laid their Lord's body.

"Why do you look for life in the place of the dead? He is not here! He is risen! Look, this is where you laid Him!"

Their faces. What was in their faces? And how did they return to the other disciples? Whatever happened to them there and later when He appeared to them, charged them with a passion that still, two thousand years later, makes us believe their story.

Sinner Saved by Grace

If you could see what I once was —
If you could go with me
Back to where I started from,
Then I know you would see
The miracle of love that took
Me in its sweet embrace
And made me what I am today —
A sinner saved by Grace.

How could I boast of anything
I've ever seen or done?
How could I dare to claim as mine
The vict'ries God has won?
Where would I be, had God not brought me
Gently to this place?
I'm here to say I'm nothing but
A sinner saved by Grace.

I'm just a sinner saved by Grace
When I stood condemned to death,
He took my place
Now I grow and breathe in freedom
with each breath of life I take;
I'm loved and forgiven —
Back with the living —
I'm just a sinner saved by Grace.

Sinner Saved by Grace

One of the many joys of our work is traveling with and coming to know and love some wonderful people. Bill says we "collect characters," and he is right. Artists are a breed all to themselves. We love them! They seem to be wired with their sensors closer to the surface than other human beings. They not only experience what happens to them, they feel what happens to other people, too.

Most of us, when we hear a great song or read great writing, say to ourselves, *Why, I could have written that!* Great artists make us feel that way. We experience what artists do; they just "tune in" and are able to express for us what we all feel and know to be true.

Artists — singers, painters, writers, communicators — are often an odd blend of the hermit (quiet lover of solitude) and the "communal animal" (who thrives on being with others). Artists get in heated discussions of deep philosophical or theological concepts. They are great storytellers and laugh at their own jokes. They cry more, laugh more, and sometimes withdraw more than most people. They swallow life in great gulps, then distill the pain and glory to "three verses and a chorus" or a play or a scene for a novel.

One of the "characters" Bill and I collected is George Younce. George is not only one of the greatest bass singers who ever slid to a low note, but he is also a great storyteller and a very funny man. When we share the stage with the Cathedral Quartet, you can be sure there will be hardy laughter coming from the "Green Room" backstage, where the singers gather before, during, and after a concert to eat snacks, drink coffee, and tell stories of the road.

George has the greatest stories and tells them with more humor than anyone we know. When George tells them, even old stories we all know by heart double us over with laughter.

Like most artists, George can be just as serious as he is funny. No one loves the stories of Jesus any better than George; nor do I know anyone who is more likely to be moved by a great song or a sincere compliment from an innocent child. George loves his Lord and he loves his family. He treasures his friends.

He loves to tell and retell the story of how God found him and changed his life. It's the story of a country boy from Mississippi who lied about his age and, in 1947, left his Christian home to join the paratroops. George tells what happened:

> Unfortunately I got in with the wrong crowd, and a boy named
> Mousey Gonzales introduced me to my first "left-handed ciga-

rette" — marijuana. I worked "special duty" as a bartender for the HCO and Officers' Club. Not only did I mix and serve drinks, I'd also sing country songs for the officers. This was not a very healthy atmosphere for a young, green country boy who had strayed from his upbringing and from the Lord. What was supposed to be only three months of special duty turned into three years of bar tending and a longer struggle with alcohol.

After George finished his tour of duty in the service, he went to Alaska, looking for adventure. But after only a few months, he returned home. He says, "I was restless and searching when one night the Lord spoke to my heart, and I realized there was no hope for me without Jesus. I got down on my knees and rededicated my life to Him, and I've never looked back."

With that commitment George let God do a work that has changed everything. "He's blessed me beyond belief!" George will tell you as he recites the beauty God has poured into his life down through the years: a family who loves God, friends all over the country who are like family, and an opportunity to travel and sing of his Redeemer for almost forty years with Glenn Payne and the other men who make up The Cathedrals.

One night after a concert that had been especially anointed by the Spirit of the Lord, George said, "The Cathedrals are going back into the studio to record soon. I'd love it if you two would write me a song. You know my story; I'm just an old sinner saved by grace." Bill and I felt honored that he asked, and we did put George's story in a song, "Sinner Saved by Grace."

If you asked George today — even after all of the awards he's received, the recordings he's made, the acclaim that's been showered on him — he would tell you he owes all he is or ever will be to a loving Father whose love would not let him go. "No wonder this song is very special to me," George told us. "The first verse expresses what is in my heart, for it was truly a 'miracle of love' that 'made me what I am today — just an old sinner, saved by grace!' I owe everything to Jesus."

Once the song was finished and recorded, we realized it was our story, too, and the story of hundreds of folks across the country who have since written to us or the Cathedrals to say, "You must have written that song just for me." Though the details may differ from story to story, we all are sinners — saved only by the wonderful grace of God.

Unshakable Kingdom

They came to follow Him,
Drawn by what He promised them
If they would sell all that they had;
He said that God would send
A kingdom that would never end
Where all the poor would be rich.
And in their discontent
They heard what they thought He meant —
Heard that the weak would be strong,
Bread would be multiplied,
Hunger be satisfied
And every servant a king.

But He went His quiet way,
Giving Himself away,
Building what eyes could never see.
While men looked for crowns and thrones,
He walked with crowds, alone,
Planting a seed in you and me —
Crying for those who cried,
Dying for those who died,
Bursting forth, glorified! Alive!
Yet some of them looked for Him,
Sad that it had to end,
But some dared to look within and see

The kingdom of God, a kingdom that would never end...
The living, unshakable kingdom of God!

Unshakable Kingdom

December 28 is Holy Innocents Day, the day set aside to remember the infants slaughtered by King Herod in an effort to kill Jesus, the prophesied King of kings. The "crime" for which these babies were put to death? They seemed to pose a threat to Herod's way of life: his throne, his power, and the deeply entrenched economic system.

Could it be that we live in a culture of Herods? These days we hear a lot about personal empowerment and "looking out for number one." We are told that we must take control of our own lives, that we are the monarchs of our own destinies. What a terrifying thought! The very idea of supremacy over circumstances mandates that other kings must die, that we may eliminate anything or anyone in the way of our control. Herod's example taught us that the hunger and thirst for supremacy demands that other kings, other lords must go.

A declaration of ultimate control is a declaration of war on others who might challenge that control. Children, babies born or unborn, husbands, wives, neighbors, aging parents — none of these must challenge our personal kingship if we are lords of our own destiny, masters of our own circumstances. No wonder as our society seeks more personal autonomy, we have more crime, more violence, more aggressive behavior, more abuse.

And how ironic that the baby who slipped through Herod's grasp and into Egypt came back riding into Jerusalem on a donkey proclaiming a kingdom established in the hearts of believers who were called to become as little children. This kingdom of children would haunt the sleep of every Herod to come until the end of time. How ironic that this manger-child survivor would declare losing to be winning, and sacrifice to be the path to resurrection.

How ironic that even those who shouted "Hosanna" and ate multiplied bread and fish on the hillside were so easily persuaded to cry "Crucify!" No wonder those who chased this Jesus with crowns and scepters and plans to force Him to greatness were the ones left holding their purple robes and golden scepters and bags of silver while He slipped away to a gnarled garden and a rugged cross to teach us what kingship is really all about.

And how ironic that both the ones who had walked with Him and the soldiers who guarded His tomb slept that Easter morning when His sealed tomb became so pregnant with glory that it burst wide open, expelling this Jesus like a newborn from the womb.

And they missed it when He gathered His friends in a circle to dance and party round a campfire on the beach, then was taken up into a cloud to return to His Father, like a child caught up with angels in a dream.

And ever since that day, those who have let His Word lodge in the fertile womb of their hearts have celebrated Holy Innocents Day with joy and longing for the revelation of an ancient kingdom that will never end.

Peace Be Still

I can feel a storm brewing,
The clouds rolling in —
Thunder rumbles beyond the hill.
The elements pause to gather their force;
The night grows unnaturally still.
Below, in the depths, the turbulence swells,
And deep in my heart swells a fear
That tears through my throat in a desperate cry —
"Oh, Lord, do you know that I'm here?"

    He says, "Peace, peace be still!"
    Lifts His hand . . . "Peace, be still."
    And like a child, the winds obey Him,
    When He says, "Peace, be still."

I know the old feeling:
I've been here before —
The same dark foreboding of fear.
When winds of the past churn up my life,
And the peace that I love disappears.
Then just when I feel the pressure so great
That my frame will be crushed by the force,
My Lord stands before me and faces the wind,
His voice echoes clear through the storm . . .

    He says, "Peace, peace be still!"
    Lifts His hand . . . "Peace, be still."
    And like a child, my heart obeys Him,
    When He says, "Peace, be still."

Peace Be Still

Most of our songs have been written out of a need to express some great truth that has altered the course of our lives and, at the time, there didn't seem to be a song to express it. This is the case with the song "Peace Be Still."

In 1985 we took a group of about ninety people from across the country to Israel. Most of these people had never met until we arrived in the Holy Land. What drew them together and to this trip was a performance of a musical we had created, "He Started the Whole World Singing." All of our traveling companions had sung this work in their local churches or community choirs and wanted to be a part of a combined choir that would perform it in the Holy Land, among the Jewish people who are and were so important to the story of the Messiah — the Messiah who brought the glory, stolen by Satan in the Garden of Eden, back into our lives.

The rehearsal was scheduled for the third evening of the trip, in a hotel in Tiberias on the Sea of Galilee. During the day, after our arrival in Tiberias, we sailed in a small ship out into the sea — or lake. In the center of the lake we stopped and turned off the motor. It was a beautiful clear day; the sea was like glass, silent except for the gentle lapping of the water against the boat. We heard the faint sounds of birds in trees far across the lake.

One end of the Sea of Galilee is embraced by hills. In these hills is a cleft, and our guide explained that during storms, this cleft functioned like a tunnel, funneling the winds right onto the shallow waters. Storms, he said, came up quickly, and smooth waters like the ones we saw could turn rough and turbulent with little notice.

Our group talked about this — how these sudden storms were so much like our lives. We might be sailing smoothly on a peaceful sea until, with little warning, unexpected turbulence could churn up our days and threaten to topple our frail barks.

We took this opportunity to read together the account from Mark 4:35–41 (RSV) of Jesus and His disciples in a boat, possibly similar to ours, on this very sea after a day of seashore ministry. Jesus was exhausted, the special kind of tired that comes from giving of oneself to people and their deep needs. The ship had barely started to move out and Jesus fell asleep on a pillow in the stern of the ship, lulled by the rhythm of the waves.

As we read we noticed purple clouds gathering behind the hills, though the sun continued to glisten on the water and the sea was as tranquil as a contented child. We could imagine, now, how the wind could begin to blow behind the hills and then, intensified as it passed through the narrow corridor between the rocks, whip onto the lake. This far from shore, we could see how dangerous this situation might be, especially with no motor — only sails and oars to resist the force of the winds and waves.

When such a storm came up, Jesus was awakened by His terrified friends. He walked to the bow of the ship, stretched out His hands, palms out like a patrolman stopping traffic. "Shhh," He whispered, not to the disciples, but to the storm. "Peace! Be still." We read from Mark: "And the wind ceased, and there was a great calm" (4:39 RSV).

That day on the Sea of Galilee we understood that the storms that blow unannounced through our very souls, intensified by the circumstances of our lives, could be stilled by His voice, too.

We sat in that boat with ninety singers, among them Sandi Patty, Steve Green, and Larnelle Harris, but we couldn't find the "right song" to express exactly what we were experiencing. Someone mentioned "The Stranger of Galilee" and several other songs about water. But this experience deserved a song of its own. There in the sunshine of the silent sea we prayed together. And we sang songs of praise and thanksgiving. But the perfect song for this experience was yet to be written.

After many more unforgettable experiences in the land of our Savior, Bill and I went home. And we carried with us images that would make their way into many songs, one of those being "Peace Be Still." Whenever we sing it, we see the cleft in the tall hills and the sea that can change and threaten without notice. And we hear a voice that speaks with quiet authority to the chaos of our day, "Peace, be still."

Tell Me

Tell me, tell me
The story of Jesus.
Tell me, tell me,
Tell me once again about His love.

Tell me that old, old story
It's my only hope and glory;
Tell me the story of Jesus.
Tell me that old, old story,
It shall be my theme in glory,
Sing to me again about His love.

I'm tired of hollow-sounding words,
I'm tired of empty promise.
Won't someone sing a simple song
Of Jesus' love?

Tell me, tell me
The story of Jesus.
Tell me, tell me,
Tell me once again about His love.

Like eagle wings, it lifts me up
Above the earth around me.
Like cool, refreshing summer rain,
It leaves me clean.

Tell Me

When I was a little girl, the small church my father pastored had green *Hymns of Devotions* songbooks. My mother made the bulletins for Sunday mornings, an innovation the parishioners — in a tiny farm community in Michigan — considered a bit formal. But eventually they came to accept that it was possible for God to work in a service that was planned ahead of time.

On Sunday night we had no bulletins, and Wednesday night prayer meeting was even more informal. In both of these services the song leader would often say, "Does anyone have a song you'd like to request?"

When this opportunity presented itself, I was ready to call out from the front seat, "Number 444!" I knew the number by heart, and I never got tired of singing my favorite hymn, "I Love to Tell the Story." The gathered faithful sang my song, but no one with more enthusiasm than I. Sometimes my mother would whisper in my year, "Not quite so loud, Honey." In my memory that song is bonded to the next part of the evening service — the testimonies of the old saints and the new converts.

"Does anyone have a testimony tonight?" my father would say, and one by one folks I knew would stand and tell stories of how God had helped them get through the past week with "victory in their hearts." The stories were real ones about daily life on the farm or at the factory or in the home. The stories told me that these people took seriously Paul's advice to the Philippians: "Don't worry about anything; instead, pray about everything; tell God your needs and don't forget to thank him for his answers. If you do this you will experience God's peace, which is far more wonderful than the human mind can understand. His peace will keep your thoughts and your hearts quiet and at rest as you trust in Christ Jesus" (Phil. 4:6–7 LB).

It's been a long time since those Wednesday night services. Our lives have grown complicated somewhere along the way. So often we find ourselves in complex discussions of various versions of theology and interpretations of Scripture. Sometimes I think the Christian community has spent so much time dissecting and analyzing the words — the Greek, the Hebrew texts, the nuances of historical and cultural intent — that we miss the Word.

I sometimes feel like the blind man Jesus healed. The analyzers of his day barraged the man with questions he couldn't answer. Finally in exasperation he told them: "I don't know whether He's good or bad. All I know is, I once was blind and now I see!"

There is a longing inside my heart to strip the Gospel of Jesus to its purest, sweetest truth. Still, like the child who sat on the front pew of that little village church, I have a passion to cry, "Won't somebody just tell me the stories of Jesus?"

The old hymn I loved then is even dearer to me now after half a century of proving the simple words of the Savior to be true in our own home, in our own lives. Its message has become so precious that we wanted to write a song for this generation that restated its truth. Bill and I believe more than ever that it is not by argument that the lost will be convinced, but by the simple story of Jesus, lived out by regular people in regular places.

> I love to tell the story of unseen things above,
> Of Jesus and His glory, of Jesus and His love.
> I love to tell the story because I know it's true;
> It satisfies my longing as nothing else can do.
>
> I love to tell the story for those who know it best
> Seem hungering and thirsting to hear it like the rest;
> And when in scenes of glory we sing a new, new song,
> 'Twill be the old, old story that I have loved so long!
>
> I love to tell the story; 'twill be my theme in glory
> To tell the old, old story of Jesus and His love.
>
> —Katherine Hankey

I Don't Belong

It's not home
Where men sell their souls
And the taste of power is sweet;
Where wrong is right
And neighbors fight
While the hungry are dyin' in the streets;
Where kids are abused,
And women are used,
The weak are crushed by the strong —
Nations gone mad,
Jesus is sad
And I don't belong.

I don't belong —
I'm goin' someday
Back to my own native land.
I don't belong
And it seems like I hear
The sound of a "Welcome Home" band.
I don't belong;
I'm a foreigner here —
Singing a sojourner's song.
I've always known
This place ain't home,
And I don't belong.

Don't belong,
But while I'm here
I'll be living like I've nothin' to lose.
And while I breathe

I'll just believe
My Lord is gonna see me through.
I'll not be deceived
By earth's make-believe —
I'll close my ears to her siren-song.
By praisin' His name —
I'm not ashamed
And I don't belong!

I belong
To a kingdom of peace
Where only love is the law;
Where children lead
And captives are freed,
And God becomes a baby on the straw.
Where dead men live
And rich men give
Their kingdoms to buy back a song.
Where sinners like me
Become royalty
And we'll all belong.

Yes, I belong
And I'm goin' someday
Home to my own native land
Where I belong,
And it seems that I hear
The sound of a "Welcome Home" band.
Yes, I'll belong —
No foreigner there
Singin' a sojourner's song;
I've always known
I'm goin' home — where I belong.

I Don't Belong

Life on the road is hard work. Contrary to what most people think, those who make their living in a portable profession do not have a life of all glamour and glory. Travel is full of inconveniences and frustrations. One needs to learn to accept disappointing cancellations and long waits in airports or in truck stops for repairs — par for the course. Sleeping in crook-necked positions while leaning against a building pillar or, if one is fortunate, a friendly shoulder; eating food you don't quite recognize; adjusting to performing the "routine of toilet" in less than convenient or sanitary surroundings — these are all part of the traveler's life.

Add to these realities the assorted artistic temperaments of a troupe grouped together because they love to sing, but not necessarily because they are compatible in other ways, and you could have the makings of a civil war. At the very least, let me say from experience, traveling together gives people ample opportunity to get to know and test the validity of each other's Christian graces. It also develops some amazing friendships and calls forth some qualities in human character that are tantamount to sainthood.

Bill and I have been traveling as a part of our work for more than thirty-five years. We have had dozens — maybe, by now, hundreds — of other artists and writers, sound engineers and technicians share station wagons, vans, motor homes, buses, and planes with us for extended periods of time. We have, in that time, known a few "stinkers," but mostly we have become well acquainted with some beautiful human beings whose confessions and professions of faith were most articulately made by the quality of their servant attitudes in the pressured and unguarded moments of life, on and off the road.

When I think of *validity,* perhaps no name comes so quickly to mind as that of Buddy Greene, with whom this song was written. Buddy is a man of God in the most practical and unpious sense. One of Bill's and my all-time favorite ways to spend the hours on the road is to engage in a deep, honest discussion of a great life issue or theological concept. The truth of the adage "iron sharpens iron" is most evident when two or more people will allow each other to agree and disagree — sometimes heatedly — on the safe soil of common respect and mutual acceptance.

Buddy Greene is one of the travelers who most loves to plumb the depths of the things of God. One road discussion with him was precipitated by an article in a newspaper about the murder and sexual abuse of a child. Buddy and I were talking about how sick the world had become and how depraved human beings can act without Jesus. That turned to a discussion of how even Christian groups seem to twist and distort the simple message of love, grace, and forgiveness Jesus came to live out for us. The "politicizing" and "culturalizing" of the Gospel as a way to polarize believers seemed to us such a contradiction of Jesus' words: "Come unto me all you who are weary and burdened, and I will give you rest."

"I feel sometimes like an alien," I eventually said to Buddy. "And I'm not so sure I even want to 'belong' in a world where babies are abused and the powerful are rewarded for misusing the weak. When we start to 'fit in' in such a world, some caution light should start to blink in our souls."

"Well, you are an alien," Buddy said. "We all are. We're strangers and pilgrims. But remember, an alien is not a person without a country. Aliens are citizens, but not of the country they are in for a while. We, too, are citizens. It's just that our citizenship isn't here."

A few miles after our discussion, I gave Buddy a lyric I had finished. He took it home and called me later. "I think I've got some music to your song," he said. "Want to hear it?"

Writers often play music or read lyrics over the phone. To the tune he'd just created, Buddy sang me the lyric I'd given him. I knew it was right. "Like a glove, Buddy!" I said when he was finished.

Buddy himself recorded the song on a recording he appropriately named "Sojourner's Song," the original title of the song. I still like that title best, though the song is now known as "I Don't Belong." I like "Sojourner's Song" because the truth is, we do belong. We are citizens. It's just that our citizenship is in another country to which we are traveling. And since this world is not our home anyway, we may as well love and give and live while we're here as if we've got nothing to lose and everything to gain.

Loving God, Loving Each Other

They pushed back from the table
To listen to His words,
His secret plan before He had to go —
"It's not complicated;
Don't need a lot of rules,
This is all you'll need to know —

It's loving God, loving each other,
Making music with my friends;
Loving God, loving each other
And the story never ends.

We tend to make it harder,
Build steeples out of stone,
Fill books with explanations of the way;
But if we'd stop and listen
And break a little bread
We would hear the Master say —

It's loving God, loving each other,
Making music with my friends;
Loving God, loving each other
And the story never ends.

Loving God, Loving Each Other

What did Jesus' friends expect? What did they think He was going to tell them that night that would prove to be His farewell Passover supper with them? Did they think He had some strategic plan to topple the Romans? Judas must have thought so — must have thought his plan to identify Jesus to authorities would force Jesus' hand, make Him get on with it and establish this new kingdom, maybe with Judas as the hero when Jesus finally realized how clever he had been.

And Peter and Andrew. Did they think He was going to lay out His plan to ferret out the graft and deception in the Jewish hierarchy and clean up the Sanhedrin staff? What about the others — Bartholomew,

Simon, James, Matthew, Thomas, Thaddaeus — did they have their minds braced for carrying out complicated instructions? *Whatever He says to us, we'll do it or die trying!* Did this thought go through their minds as they waited for His words?

Through Moses they had been given the Ten Commandments, and the Levitical priests had turned those laws into a complex system of rights and restrictions for carrying out God's demands. Surely Jesus also would leave them with instructions. In their hearts they knew they might fail Him. The law they already had was impossible to keep; had it not been for the sacrifices that covered their failures, they would never have been able to maintain the standard.

After the symbolic Seder supper, Jesus picked up a loaf of unleavened bread and broke it. "This is my body which is broken for you," He said, and began to pass the broken pieces to them. Then He took the cup — not the cup He'd been using throughout the meal, but more likely the cup every Jewish boy had been forbidden to touch, the cup that sat untouched in the center of every Passover table, the Messiah's cup, Elijah's cup.

They caught their breath when He picked it up. "This," He said, "is my blood that is shed for you." Then He made reference to the cup of joy, just as every Jewish father always did throughout the meal as the wine was sipped after each traditional question. But He wasn't asking them to "sip." "Drink ye all of it," He commanded with a tone in His voice they couldn't quite identify. "Drink it that your joy may be full!"

Then He began talking about going away and how short was the time they had together, about how dear they were to Him, and how He had kept them together in the Father's name. He told them His going

away would be good for them, that He would send someone even better — "the Comforter," who would teach them all things.

"A new commandment, I give to you." His tone had changed again.

Here it comes, they probably thought, *the hard part, the complicated part,
beyond Moses and all the laws we already have to remember.*

They couldn't believe their ears at what He said next. It was almost
a letdown, and yet it was more like a relief.

"Love each other."

That was it? That was the "new commandment"? They waited for
more. But that was it. He said, "As the Father has loved me, so have I
loved you. Now, you. Love each other like that."

Then He made it clear that He considered them equals, siblings of
sorts. "I won't call you servants," He said, "because servants have no
idea what the Master is doing. Instead, I have called you friends,
because I have let you in on everything I've learned from My Father."

And then He said it again. "Love one another." Then He wanted
them to sing together one last time. There He was — on His way to
Gethsemane and on to Calvary — and He was making music with His
friends.

They would never be able to forget this night as long as they lived.
He had reduced all the laws and all the prophets' predictions and all of
the religious expectations to three things: Love God. Love each other.
Make music with all those who are My friends.

Then He walked to a cross and showed them how to love as the
Father had loved. It wasn't until Sunday morning that they realized
what He had meant about the joy and the cup. Mary came running to
tell them. Love like that which He had commanded and then modeled

had mysteriously infused everything with joy. "He's alive!" she was shouting as she banged on the locked gate. Her face shone like the sun and, like the sun that first day of a new week, He Himself had risen.

This new commandment may have been simple, but it was powerful! It had conquered death; it had made things new. It was making them new and willing to risk loving, too. They would start by loving each other, just as He'd said. And the song He'd wanted to sing would be a story-song, a story that would never end. The joy, the song, the kingdom of God. It was all the same thing and it was — in them! Not on this hill, not on that hill, but in them! They would be the living stones, and He — they'd heard Him say it — He would be the cornerstone that the builders rejected, the stone hewn out of a mountain that would fill the whole earth.

Since that night in the Upper Room when Jesus gave His disciples the simple gospel of love, many have tried to add to it and amend it, organize it and section it off, make it exclusive and establish systems of requirements. But when an honest soul can get still before the living Christ, we can still hear Him say simply and clearly, "Love the Lord your God with all your heart and with all your soul and with all your mind. . . . and love one another as I have loved you." Then as Paul wrote to the Colossians, "Sing, sing your hearts out to God!" (Col. 3:16 THE MESSAGE). It doesn't get any better — or simpler — than that!

Credits

The following are reprinted with permission of the copyright holders:

"Because He Lives," lyric by Gloria Gaither and William J. Gaither, music by William J. Gaither, Copyright © 1971, 1979 by William J. Gaither.

"Broken and Spilled Out," lyric by Gloria Gaither, music by Bill George, Copyright © 1984 by Gaither Music Company and Yellow House Music.

"The Church Triumphant," lyric by Gloria Gaither and William J. Gaither, music by William J. Gaither, Copyright © 1973 by William J. Gaither.

"The Family of God," lyric by Gloria Gaither and William J. Gaither, music by William J. Gaither, Copyright © 1970 by William J. Gaither.

"Fully Alive," lyric by Gloria Gaither, music by William J. Gaither, Copyright © 1983 by Gaither Music Company.

"Gentle Shepherd," lyric by Gloria Gaither, music by William J. Gaither, Copyright © 1974, 1975 by William J. Gaither; with "The Shepherd Friend," by Dorothy Sickal, from *Hands Across the Seasons*, Copyright © 1988 by Gaither Music Company.

"Go Ask," lyric by Gloria Gaither, music by William J. Gaither, Copyright © 1981 by Gaither Music Company.

"God Gave the Song," lyric by Gloria Gaither, William J. Gaither, and Ronn Huff; music by William J. Gaither and Ronn Huff, Copyright © 1969 by Gaither Music Company and Paragon Music Corp.

"Going Home," lyric by Gloria Gaither and William J. Gaither, music by William J. Gaither, Copyright © 1967 by William J. Gaither.

"He Touched Me," lyric and music by William J. Gaither, Copyright © 1963, 1964 by William J. Gaither.

"I Am Loved," lyric by Gloria Gaither and William J. Gaither, music by William J. Gaither, Copyright © 1978 by William J. Gaither.

"I Believe in a Hill Called Mount Calvary," lyric by Gloria Gaither, William J. Gaither, and Dale Oldham; music by William J. Gaither, Copyright © 1968 by William J. Gaither.

"I Could Never Outlove the Lord," lyric by Gloria Gaither and William J. Gaither, music by William J. Gaither, Copyright © 1972 by William J. Gaither.

"I Don't Belong," lyric by Gloria Gaither, music by Buddy Greene, Copyright © 1990 by Gaither Music Company, Rufus Music, and Spirit Quest Music.

"It Is Finished," lyric by Gloria Gaither and William J. Gaither, music by William J. Gaither, Copyright © 1976 by William J. Gaither.

"It's Beginning to Rain," lyric by Gloria Gaither and Aaron Wilburn, music by William J. Gaither and Aaron Wilburn, Copyright © 1979, 1980 by William J. Gaither and First Monday Music.

"I've Just Seen Jesus," lyric by Gloria Gaither, music by William J. Gaither and Danny Daniels, Copyright © 1984 by Gaither Music Company and Ariose Music.

"Jesus Is Lord of All," lyric by Gloria Gaither and William J. Gaither, music by William J. Gaither, Copyright © 1973 by William J. Gaither.

"Joy Comes in the Morning," lyric by Gloria Gaither and William J. Gaither, music by William J. Gaither, Copyright © 1974 by William J. Gaither.

"The King Is Coming," lyric by Gloria Gaither and William J. Gaither, last verse in part by Charles Millhuff; music by William J. Gaither, Copyright © 1970 by William J. Gaither.